THE HOLLYWOOD HALLUCINATION

by

Parker Tyler

Introduction by
RICHARD SCHICKEL

SIMON AND SCHUSTER
NEW YORK

Certain material used in the chapter "The Good Villain
and the Bad Hero" originally appeared under different
form in View.

INTRODUCTION

As a reader I am peculiarly, indeed fatally, attracted to the special kind of critical daring practiced by Parker Tyler in *The Hollywood Hallucination* and *Magic and Myth of the Movies*. This daring consists of two major elements: a willingness to risk overinterpretation of specific objects (the popular films and film stars that catch his endlessly roving eye) and the courage to build on these fragile and transitory creations a towering theoretical structure (a structure from which, it should be added, one can gain a unique view of the way one of our most significant cultural institutions actually works—or used to work at the height of its powers—on us). There are a few works of literary criticism that are a little bit like Mr. Tyler's books; one thinks of Lawrence's *Studies in Classic American Literature*, Pound's *ABC of Reading*, Fiedler's *Love and Death in the American Novel*. But it requires a very commodious critical tradition, much critical activity, to produce even such a small number of stimulating, intelligently eccentric works. We have not had, in film criticism, anything like the level of activity, or length of history, that can support such work. Indeed, there has been so little basic scholarly activity in film (a situation now, perhaps, beginning to be rectified), so little genuine criticism (as opposed to reviewing), that it is a wonder we have produced even the tiny, standard shelf of worthwhile volumes we now have (*Agee on Film*, Warshow's *The Immediate Experience*, Kael's *I Lost It at the Movies*, and three or four others).

It has long been my contention that Mr. Tyler's two books

belong in that select company and that they are the more remarkable in that they were published in 1944 and 1947. For at that time a man attempting to seriously comprehend the phenomenon of film was really working on his own, with no tradition to sustain him, few books and articles to refer to, few colleagues with whom he might conversationally test and refine his ideas. And, worse, as the indifferent commercial reception of these books proved, no genuine audience to address—just a handful of fellow buffs, nuts, fans . . . you pick the patronizing word.

Indeed, it is as some such character that Mr. Tyler was brought to the attention of the nonspecialist audience recently, when Gore Vidal, in the course of his extended sick joke, *Myra Breckinridge*, seized on *Magic and Myth* as just the kind of work—so intense it often comes close to self-parody—his hero–heroine–whatchamacallit required as motivation-inspiration for his–her–its idiot savantry about Hollywood. If Mr. Tyler's book had not existed, Vidal would have had to invent it.

And, in decency, he should have. Except that he couldn't have, for there is nothing in his work with the imaginative intensity, the intellectual daring, of Mr. Tyler's work. I am sure the subject is, or was, painful to Mr. Tyler, since undoubtedly large numbers of the reading public now think of him as an invention of Vidal's. On the other hand, there is no critic in America better equipped to understand and appreciate the irony of this transformation of himself from a living reality into a symbolic fiction.

Indeed, it is one of the basic ironies he explores in these two books. All the movie stars he writes about preceded him in the kind of self-transcendence Vidal foisted on him. Creators of images (usually unconsciously, since they have the fortune or misfortune of looking like our imagined ideal of hero or villain, vamp or virgin), they become prisoners of those images. They come to each new role with bits of gossip about their private selves adhering to their public selves, trailing the bright rags and tatters of previous impersonations, encumbered by our expectations about what the behavior of certain types ought to be in certain situations. So they become creatures at once less than human and more than human. It is Mr. Tyler's prime business to explicate the iconography of these faces and forms—more real than real at first glance, less and less so the more we study them—and it is singular that, a quarter century after he introduced us to the fascinating possibilities inherent in this work, he has found so few disciples. For once we begin tracing out such analyses with him it seems a completely logical, completely natural thing to do.

And so it also is when he begins to work on the cliché that movies are dreams, the studios, dream factories. It is, he argues, in the nature of a camera designed to capture *moving* images to create a special kind of realism—surrealism—a special kind of naturalism—supernaturalism. But it is not just technics that impart this quality to movies. There is also the industry as social, commercial institution to consider. With its "mad search for novelty, the iron necessity to keep producing and to find ideas, angles," it unconsciously contrives to create a much richer matrix of meanings—and ambiguities—than, to use Mr. Tyler's example, "the efforts of dramatists to congregate enough words . . . to permit the curtain to ring down on another Broadway hit" can possibly aspire to. In other words, the drama clearly visible within the borders of the screen does not end there. He alludes to the off-screen drama, much more intense, that may take place between a directorial Svengali and his current Trilby. He mentions how an actor's vocal quality, his accent, may work against the characterization he strives for, may work for it, but always "refuses to be completely absorbed into the artistic mesh and creates a little theater of its own." The attempts to shoehorn "properties" into preexisting mythopoetic screen forms produce yet another interesting example of off-screen tension that is scarcely ever mentioned in formal reviews, yet is acknowledged in the trade phrase "licking the story" (rather as a mother cat licks her newborn offspring into acceptable behavioral patterns), and in our minds as we witness the movie unfolding before us. And then there is the career drama proceeding in almost every film we ever see. For example, Jennifer Jones in *The Song of Bernadette* asking us, after her "novitiate" in B westerns for "strict observance of the occasion" of her arrival in major films, like "a trained nurse admonishing us with finger on lips and murmuring: 'actress winning award.'" And so much, much more that Tyler himself can say better than an emcee can.

What it comes to, in essence, is this: There is the conscious movie: the one the people who created it thought they were making and the one we thought we were paying our way in to see. Then there is the unconscious movie: the one neither makers nor viewers are consciously aware of, a movie that exposes the attitudes, neuroses, desires shared by both parties. This film, if not beyond good and evil, is certainly beyond the reach of "good" reviews or "bad" reviews, beyond favorable or unfavorable criticism. It is not, however, beyond contemplation of the sort Mr. Tyler practices.

And, it should be mentioned, his style is as unique as his subject matter. He has a way of warily circling his prey, surrounding it with speculation, until, weary and frightened by an astute hunter, it falls victim to one of his quick dashes to its most vulnerable point.

I said at the beginning that I am extremely vulnerable to the charm of daring critical huntsmen of Mr. Tyler's sort, inclined to concede them their excesses of enthusiasm, their occasional lapses (even into incomprehensibility). Implicit in their enterprise is their own vulnerability to satirical and parodistical shots of the sort that people like Vidal, with their unquestioned ability to hit the broad side of a barn, can so easily make. Most of the best screen actors and screenplays, the ones we best and most lovingly remember, are similarly vulnerable, as is much of our best literature. In the end, work of this kind lingers in the mind precisely because it opens it up, leaves it speculating, trying to apply radical formulations to new phenomena as they appear.

It is possible, of course, that some of my affectionate regard for Mr. Tyler's work stems from the fact that most of his examples are drawn from a period (the late Thirties and the Forties) that happened to be the most formative one for me as a watcher in the shadows. They may seem obscure or distant to people under thirty-fivish. Yet, most of the genres and performer types he discusses are still very much with us. And the processes by which they were created are still very much alive and well wherever people get together and make movies. Styles may change but the basics remain constant. Mr. Tyler may have written these books as the sound film passed through adolescence—age 14–18—but the bending of the twig was by then complete and its maturity was clearly prefigured. And even if the New American Film that one now sees taking shape should totally drive the traditional commercial product from the screen (which I doubt, some form of coexistence being a much better bet) *The Hollywood Hallucination* and *Magic and Myth of the Movies* would remain essential tools for understanding film history. Moreover, the mark they have made on at least some writers about film since they were published would remain indelible, even if, as is generally the case, unacknowledged.

Movies are, no matter what else they may from time to time claim to be, a mythopoetic form, and Mr. Tyler's criticism has, appropriately enough, a poetic quality about it. The critic Barbara Herrnstein Smith has lately defined the poem as an entity which "allows us to know what we know, including our illusions and desires, by giving us the language in which to acknowledge it." That, precisely, is what Mr.

Tyler was trying to do when he wrote in his strange, compelling, uniquely rewarding way about films back in the days when we knew no better than to call them "the movies" and pretend their unimportance to us.

RICHARD SCHICKEL

CONTENTS

To the memory of my mother,
that golden nature whose image so often
illuminated with me this side of the movie screen.

CHAPTER I

THE PLAY IS NOT THE THING

In Hollywood, anything but the play is usually the thing. Whereas the tradition of the legitimate theater conceives presentation as a sort of centripetal operation, all forces tending toward the center of a single artistic inspiration and directly deriving their character from contact with it, the genius of Hollywood has progressively opposed such a conception and tended centrifugally to regard the story as but a jumping-off place for a complex series of superimposed and often highly irrelevant operations. The process which a novel or play, contemporary or historic, must go through before it reaches a movie audience is familiar enough. It is a bromide of Hollywood that hundreds of thousands of dollars may be paid for a title alone, a title of course which has been attached to a Broadway hit or a best-selling book. *Foreign Correspondent,* by Vincent Sheean, and *The Company She Keeps,* by Mary McCarthy, are notable cases in point. Irreverence in this sense has been the bible of the movie city. Nonetheless, the loud and infinite clink of cinema dollars has overwhelmed the still, small voice of the proud author, who has been known to exclaim publicly that he fails to recognize the child of his imagination. The point is, he recognizes only too well the distortions, from the casting to the dialogue, but finds it necessary to deny parenthood in order to save his face. But his face has been irretrievably lost; indeed, it is now the face of Norma Shearer or Joan Bennett, and as such it must inevitably go down among the optical archives to posterity.

The voice of the proud author is not only still but still small; on the other hand, especially of recent times, there are exceptions to the rule that authors are tempted to repudiate their works after transference to the screen. Moreover, the widening scope of the movie industry has progressively allowed for the "fine" exceptions, promoting a reciprocal graciousness between literature and the cinema. Two outstanding examples, *The Informer* and *How Green Was My Valley*, came from the same director, John Ford. It is difficult to determine exactly what turns the scales in favor of the original literary conception; sometimes, it is an insistent author, one who contracts to take a personal interest in Hollywood machinations. It is not that Hollywood is always unwilling to collaborate with

authors; often certain ones, such as Ben Hecht and
Clifford Odets, already crowned (however dubiously)
with artistic laurels, are seduced into employment as
script and scenario and dialogue writers, causing literature and cinema to become hand-in-glove conspirators
against ultimately embarrassing discrepancies—not
only between the written word and the screen image
but between the written word and "life."

Sentimental worshipers of the written word are often
great enough in number to overawe any original impulses of presentation that may occur to an omnipotent
mind of the movie industry; the readers of *Gone with
the Wind* stood like a vast jury at the gates of Hollywood, prepared to judge even the candidates for the
rôles of Scarlett O'Hara and Rhett Butler. Of course,
the jury were summoned by the penetrating whisper of
the publicity department, but they appeared with the
obedient alacrity of a geni rubbed in his most sensitive
spot. Thus—so uneven is the administration of the
movie capital—it is possible to exploit optional slavery
to the written word, as such a thing of itself may seem
sensational.

The question of Hollywood's judgment, its strategy
in regard to the evaluative scale placed upon what it
buys or selects from the grab bag of the past—as it
selected *Romeo and Juliet*—leads to the very heart of
American cinematic matter. Does a principle of selection exist? And, furthermore, why has Hollywood

never developed an original literature, a definite script-character of its own, entirely without dependence upon the stage or "literature"?

I believe the answer to the corollary question can be grasped intuitively: Because, being a vast attempt to industrialize an artistic medium, Hollywood must feed upon all sorts of digestive devices and an agglomeration of raw materials to satisfy its mere size. It is mammoth, mammal, mammon. Theoretically, there is nothing which the camera cannot conceive and project on a conveniently empty screen; nothing, from journalism to Shakespeare; and there is nothing, practically, which it leaves untouched. Hollywood cannot be choosy. Its methods are those of a superlatively equipped factory prepared to transform anything according to a flexible method of manufacture. It does not matter if *taint* is present in the material; it can be refined or eliminated; if *taint* is lacking and deemed necessary, Hollywood creates its own peculiar taint, which shows in the finished article like silver threads in an evening gown on Claudette Colbert.

As Entrepreneur of Anything, Hollywood is inevitably a popular institution, and its sins of omission are the normal ones of such an institution. Built upon an extensive rather than an intensive scale of operations, it tends to sacrifice what is unique and take second- or third-hand what is original. Its studios are like a continuous cell-structure all in the same organism, but capable of anything at any moment, held together only by an established preoccupation with a single mechanical instrument, the camera. More than a camel has passed into the heaven of America's movie houses through this "needle's eye." Apparitions known and unknown, from Frankenstein's monster to Mr. Hyde, from Snow White to Dumbo, from Fatty Arbuckle and Zasu Pitts to Mae West and Garbo doing the rumba. For one reason or another, often superficial but sometimes of profound interest, each of them has been appropriate, and arrived with no pain attached to their wonderful uterine passage.

What, then, of the principle of selection? It must be either phony or practically invisible. But it is too powerful to be phony and too egregious to be totally invisible. Any tangible dynamic has its lurking law, its rudiment of choice, and that of Hollywood has the curiously protean law of a *centrifugal collective*. Its selectivity is thus hazardous and dialectical. It does not revolve about a static original scheme (as Maurice Evans and company revolved about the uncut *Hamlet*); any given Hollywood periphery, whether it be Broadway-laid Shakespeare, such as *The Boys from Syracuse*, or a studio writer's pristine inspiration, is "cubistic" in character. Once an original story or idea is bought and delivered (here the term "original" is acutely accurate), its subtle and often semi-conscious process of transformation begins.

The "idea" may go through three or four script and scenario writers, its preparation meanwhile being supervised by the star, the director, and the producer, who eventually must also approve it. Then the actual "shooting" begins—in which are involved not only the actors but the supervisor of production, the director, the assistant director, the camera man, and the assistant camera man. During the shooting occur the test showings, which lead to a certain number of "retakes" (scenes photographed again); these may lead even to a change of plot or casting. The final product must go through the cutting room, and the film-editor, whose importance is not usually understood by audiences, assumes his place in the scheme. It is an axiom of the industry that this man may make or almost be allowed to break a picture. Thus a single movie is as highly departmentalized as the most cellular of bureaucracies—only its endeavors are directed toward a creative rather than a mere formal or routine result. If often Hollywood's results are formal and routine, it is owing to the operation of a wide and elastic metaphysic: the instinct of the producers to please an almost illimitable public.

It is said, and truthfully, that much of the organization of a movie depends upon the director, but his authority fluctuates. There are a number of talented directors powerful enough to affect and even control almost all aspects of production, but (even putting aside the notion that his "free hand" may be due to his having made early, important compromises) for him to get a unified result, he must constantly apply his will. There is usually some point at which he is forced to give in, either from ennui, fear, or discretion, to the demands of others. This is notably the experience of directors imported from abroad. Such men have been in much greater control of their productions on foreign soil for the simple reason that bureaucratization there has been more primitive, as the economic structure of the industry was simpler. But another cause was the tradition of respect for the "original script," of which the director has been the commanding representative. The foreign directors have found that they are up against something bigger than the mere problem of giving a story a cinematic form. Besides the general unwieldiness of Hollywood production machinery (so far as unity of purpose goes), the star is sometimes more powerful than the director, and may have different ideas. Being bossed primarily by the producer, who is very seldom the director in America, the star makes a complaint, and so on. Von Stroheim, a foreign director domesticated before any of the others, was notorious for his egotism and waywardness, and his expenditures on production seldom were redeemed in terms of financial profit to his backers. Whenever he prevailed, someone was bound to be sorry—usually too sorry.

Yet no one can be made *too* unhappy because of Hollywood: this is to be taken axiomatically. The complex machine of the movie industry may be termed roundly a collective phenomenon in which is imbedded a will to make indiscriminate numbers of people indiscriminately happy. Written on the walls of Griffith's Babylon, as well as on those of Darryl Zanuck's and Samuel Goldwyn's offices, were and are, in invisible ink, the words: *Take thy neighbor's advice —it is bound to be worth something to someone. But be sure first that he is paid a large salary; this makes him generous of advice.* It is strange: the degree to which one is tempted to seek the secret of so extraordinary an organism as Hollywood, as though one searched for the soul of the mechanical Frankenstein . . .

The focal point of Hollywood dynamics is a kind of material workroom into which is introduced the germ of a narrative idea. Since it is a brain capable of extending its operations in space, it grows with the dimensions of its own ideas, involving its energy factors quantitatively, and thus evolving its original "idea" in quality as it amplifies it in quantity. That is why even a Shakespearean play is reduced to the fetus-state within the walls of Hollywood. This *individuality* of the type of growth is the movie capital's vanity and triumph. Hollywood is in the nature of things because it adds to that nature. The purely logical origin of its contribution lies solely in the remarkable capacity of the movie camera to transcend stage effects.

Literature in the movies has assumed a minor rôle precisely in ratio to the increase of technical cinema effects. At first sight, this may seem a contradictory statement, inasmuch as "serious" literature has gotten a bigger break as the industry has "come of age." But coming of age is a relative convention. How seriously has serious literature ever been taken in Hollywood? Indeed, in certain respects, Hollywood has become less serious just where it might have been expected, because of amplitude of means, to become more serious. It may not be quite a platitude to declare that Hollywood's waywardness is due to intoxication with its technical powers in the giddy springtime of those powers. In this way it is at once as naïve and sophisticated as Frankenstein's monster—depending upon which end of the human-mechanical scale you look at it. As a machine, it is wonderfully human; as humanity, it is awesomely mechanical.

Hollywood is nothing if not a show-off. And what is showing off but the will toward form regardless of content, the impulse toward expression regardless of skill? Hollywood's awkwardness balances its tour de force. An acrobat, a conceited child, a machine are all show-offs. The muscular expenditure in which not even a race is won . . . the fluorescence of sauciness that turns out childish jabberwocky . . . the precise and monotonous operation regardless of grist—all these modes are in the same series of psychological dynamics. Any one of the operations may please or irritate, according to the occasion, the psychology of the observer, or the skill of the performer. But the primary point about the "show-off" is that his effort is in a sense its own reward, and depends only relatively upon the result observed in the spectator, or any other "objective" criterion. The psychology of show-offism is independent self-consciousness: a trying-out of powers for their own benefit: a narcissism of energy. And here is the most subtle part of Hollywood dynamics: the implicit but necessary rôle of the narcissistic movies is to let as many people as possible "in on" its narcissism, which is only the showing-off by the camera; it is to give the assembled spectators the *illusion* of their own technical virtuosity. That is why the screen is in more than a simple sense a mirror. It is a psychologically cubistic mirror in which dimension is materially reproduced or "reflected" in the texture of the psychological medium itself—that texture being the collectivity of the artistic creators, the cinema craftsmen, as an unusually intelligent bureaucracy.

Thus, representational taste and creative judgment in Hollywood cannot be standardized or conveniently isolated as formal means. Form, in the purely esthetic sense, is the deliberate and controlled imprint of a single intelligence on a certain material and is the only means by which we dare approach this material. Obviously, the form of Hollywood, relating so much to current fashions and to popular show-offism, must be in a fundamentally impotent and perpetually liquescent state. Such a super-plasticity has its drawbacks in respect to the esthetic relation between form and content.

There comes to mind a classic of the silent days starring Theda Bara and called A Fool There Was. It illustrates very well the difference in tone between a "serious" latter-day drama and one of yesterday. The material of the Bara film is obviously third-rate from an artistic viewpoint, but most impressive, when I saw it again three years ago, was the concentration upon a serious aspect of human emotion: a disintegrating erotic passion. As lurid and obvious a conception as the Vampire was, she was more serious, both morally and artistically, than Bette Davis' neurotic or Garbo's exotic woman. It is true that Garbo acted a Tolstoi, a Dumas, and a Pirandello heroine, but in proportion as the screen had more camera angles, lighting devices, scenic effects, and narrative tricks to exploit, the theme—and the way character emphasizes theme—lost value in these Garbo pictures. As a result, her Camille became a dextrous series of familiar Garbo postures, intonations, and swoons, ending in the greatest swoon of cinema history: Camille's death-bed scene. Though Theda Bara was soon converted into

the leading siren of her day as Garbo of this, it is on
the contrary *the theme* which remains uppermost in
A Fool There Was, her first picture. At that time, the
camera had a definite reportorial humility; it was
present to record the main objective events, and this
film had an almost Flaubertian simplicity of plot. The
wife is chaste and futile; the Vampire is corrupt and
triumphant; the faithless husband is weak and doomed
—as the picture proceeds, they become more so. The
camera then had not become a virtuoso in its own
right; its logic was simple since its capacity was limited, its field barren of elaborate effects. Until Griffith
exploited the intimacy of the close-up, it even stood,
so to speak, at a respectful distance from the actor, but
thereafter emotions began to be more intimate, more
fugitive. Even the pioneering Griffith was relatively
simple in his psychology and thus in his cinematic
logic. When he thought of great events, such as the
panorama of the past, of the heyday and destruction
of cultures, priests, and kings, he thought of vast
spaces and vast sets, and photographed them as
though they were the Grand Canyon, allowing the
camera to approach "at its own peril."

Today a "great event" in Hollywood is indiscriminately a "wow" close-up of Dietrich, a grab of a
coveted copyright, the importation of a foreign actor,
someone's divorce, or a prop set of a city: a masterpiece of illusion. A profound relativity of size has in-

vaded and dominated the precincts of Hollywood "artistic morality," no less than Hollywood studios. Since the industry is big, every detail, which is so important as a link in the whole machine, is also big; but so aggressive is the Hollywood dynamic that such "details" or departments tend to overexpand and assume an individualistic hallucination of the whole. The movie city entertains a strange mathematics: *the whole is equal to less than the sum of all its parts.*

Each studio department is subconsciously out for itself, and wants to shine as independently as possible in Movie Heaven. Many a shot is a kind of three-ring circus, a contest for attention between the make-up man, the dialogue writer, and the star's personality. In particular, the rôle of make-up is insidiously introduced. When Lon Chaney, the exotic character man of American cinematic history, used make-up, it was to exploit its sensational effects; thus the artificiality was as easy to take as it was obvious. But Paul Muni's make-up is the modest—and thus carefully immodest —attribute of a virtuoso who desires only to seem inconspicuous, commonplace. Why, then, can we never quite forget that Mr. Muni is wearing an elaborate make-up? Only because he is even more anxious than we are to conceal the fact by his perfect nonchalance. But why is he so patently *nonchalant?* Because he, as the star, is more important than the story, and knows it. The feeling of consciously "hogging" the camera is communicated by numbers of Hollywood actors, and Mr. Muni, even as a European, was noted for making love to the spotlight. Such was the esthetic error in *Zola*: it was not a *play*, it was a biographical sketch of a man called Emile Zola who once imagined, a little absurdly, that he was Paul Muni. The reason that the same effect almost never occurs in foreign films is that foreign actors are bred in a tradition of subordination to character, which in turn is subordinated to story—namely, to a single artistic conception which is all that a play is. No Hollywood actor, however, dares to subordinate himself in theory to anything, and of course his director follows this rule of actor-hegemony pretty closely. No one in the industry can stop striving a minute, for if he does, someone or *something* may steal the scene or the picture from under his nose. I have often sat luxuriating and lazy in my seat, watching with relish the metaphysical sweat of American movie actors, especially Clark Gable and Spencer Tracy, doing their darnedest to outact Donald Duck and Dumbo a few blocks away. And what can tell us better than the lips of Rita Hayworth and Ann Sheridan, pronouncers of special dialogue by special writers, that the play is not the thing in Hollywood?

Hollywood is strong enough to transcend "the play." Yet it is important to determine what, in essence, and as an indivisible visual-literary product it is which the

Factory City of Fancy offers in the guise of a play. The answer is simpler than it may seem: *the charade.* In a charade, a word is guessed by observing a pantomimic scheme improvised by human performers for representing its syllables. Of course, the actors in a cinema charade are given the solution, "the word," in advance, but the point is they have to employ the pantomimic-literary system of symbols provided by the scenarist—and there's the catch. One can imagine, after recalling all I have said about the creative machinery of Hollywood, what the problems of a charade-provider must be. The hazards which may befall his interpretation of a given theme or plot may be manifold and relatively catastrophic. It is not inconceivable that a charade may come full-blown into the head of an idea-man, for popular fiction in magazines and books is likewise on a perpetual production basis vulgarizing ideas and parodying social reality. Indeed, a cinema charade is sometimes only a parody of a freely circulating theme in current fiction.

The actor himself—a point which will be brought out in the following chapters—is always able, since his art is one of individualistic competition and monopolistic rigor, to impose a charade on a charade. Great stars are accustomed to step into rôles adapted for them in advance; their idiom has already been imposed upon the material selected by the idea department.

Thus a scenarist's "trained incapacity" for understanding the drama or novel material with which he is presented is further complicated by the star's "trained incapacity" for acting any but one rôle, one human type, whether it be close to average life or far from it. Thus the Hollywood star-system tends toward monolithism of idea, interrupting this motion only when (another of the industry's stunts) four top-ranking players are cast all in one film to see if more than two make a crowd at the box office.

Till very recently, it would have been far from an original observation that the most dependable money-makers are the star-personalities to whom the art of portrayal and the art of drama are the most remote considerations. At the moment, some of the perennial features of movie-manufacture are bogging down, an eventuation not altogether due to universal social convulsions. Finally, it is the charade stereotype which has proved most perduring, and a short analysis will demonstrate the reason for such hardihood. Since, in a charade, the action must be extremely simple and commonplace so that the game can proceed quickly, the basic idea must pertain to a single word or two or three words. Moreover, the action of the performers sometimes combines crude elements of symbolism with its realism because, as a rule, actual objects are excluded from the pantomime. Accordingly, the relation of *charade* to *reality* is indefinitely oblique, almost like the relation of a child's primer to adult language, whereas the reality is that of presumably grown-up folk. Thus the correlation between thought and action is not only of a primitive logic, but highly approximate. Approximateness is the distinguishing quality of the relation between the basic plot-idea, which the audience instinctively associates with reality, and the pantomimic plot which Hollywood designs to portray "reality." The basic idea therefore has to become even more elementary than it was in the beginning to be brought within touching distance of communication by movie technique. An illustration of this was in the "normashearing" of *Romeo and Juliet*, in which the feud between the Montagues and the Capulets needed only Jimmie Durante for it to seem like a skit from *Jumbo*. Then, if the myth-pattern be that of a great star, such as Dietrich or Garbo, the plot-dimensions shrink nakedly without shame and assume a charade silhouette in the eyes of the beholder. Details become inconsequential, realism is dissolved in the alembic of heterogeneous, more or less stupid, artifices.

If this esthetic reaction to hundreds of Hollywood products is not common to movie-goers, it is only because of the supreme transcendence of Hollywood entertainment power. This power is in the fun, the plain lack of literary seriousness of the cinema charade, effected by its use of all manner of tours de force. The more consciously funny Hollywood is, the less chance it has of being unconsciously funny or incongruous, as it so often and so subtly is. A peculiar irony of this law is that the Hollywood actor, and particularly actress, who sometimes have an inferiority complex toward more serious players, appear to be condescending toward the comic idiom when doing comedy. It is usually hard to say whether this is from simple lack of sensibility or due to hard perversity. So many little complexes appear like jewels on the wrists of Hollywood ladies! I call to mind Joan Crawford's *nostalgia for tragedy* in the romantic comedy, *When Ladies Meet*.

Such defects are no more solely the personal fault of actors than any other idiosyncrasy which Hollywood may call its own. First and last comes the movie capital's protean energy, fixed and yet flowing. It is this American city's monumentally practiced delusion of grandeur with which I am concerned in this book, which I certainly have not undertaken merely to analyze the failure of its industry to create the unity of a work of art. From one viewpoint, the energy of Hollywood must be called *super-artistic*. At the same time, its power of presenting *the real*—the illusion of the real—is so great that effects flow from it which engulf the beholder (and I confess I am one such) in a maze of symbolic emotions. These emotions are not logically formalized on the screen, but issue from it in free forms that seduce and entangle by their universal repercussiveness. Like a watchful comet, art in Hollywood awaits its chance to shine, shedding perennially a *dialectical* kind of light, illuminating as much by its bad taste and illogicality—indeed, illuminating more by these than by its isolated triumphs.

CHAPTER II

HOLLYWOOD'S SURREALIST EYE

Dısplacement, so familiar and democratic in surrealism and dreams, is the unofficial, veiled dictator of Hollywood. In this way, the movie city is being true to its own deep tradition. When pictures first moved, the photographer showed off their virtuosity by imitating the visual illusions of magicians—displacement of the kind practiced by sleight-of-hand artists. But the original delight-in-displacement has traveled a long road, one strewn with the "corpses" of the technical advances of the cinema. Museums, such as the Museum of Modern Art Film Library in New York City, hold the documents tracing this advance, though one might say that on the surface, at least, they are placements rather than displacements; and just in the sporting sense, like an ace-shot in tennis which somehow suggests a perfect "close-up," or the cinematic angleshot which displaces the normal point of vision and obtains a view unexpected of the circumstances. And there is the "swimming close-up": an eye that moves through the air with the greatest of ease, as supple as a fish in dodging the obstacles between it and the climax of its passage; one such in *Citizen Kane* goes through electric signs and past the glass of a skylight to settle its cold nose against the heroine's cheek.

As a recorder and creator of movement, the movie camera has been inevitably an instrument capable of as much displacing as placing, as much alienation as familiarizing. In moving with a more pyrotechnic virtuosity than the human eye, it has displaced *the body* of the spectator and rendered it, as a carriage of perception, fluid; the eye itself has become a body capable of greater spatial elasticity than the human body, insofar as it seems a sort of detachable organ of the body. By turning one's head, one can accomplish much more in scope of perception than the movie camera, being able to see more, as they say, "at one glance." But one does not add to the clarity of that perception excepting through the limited devices of the telescope and microscope. These very instruments demonstrate that *clarity* of vision is largely a question of *attention* and thus of exclusion, narrowing. It remains for the peculiarly *alienating* faculty of the movie camera to clarify and "selectify" vision in a generally significant sense. Was it not possible to see *at one glance* the most extraordinary possibilities in such an art-medium? Was the camera not a kind of monster capable of projecting marvels? Mechanical marvels, when they have appeared, have become commonplaces, but some of them manage to retain permanently the faculty of creating the wonderful.

The very soul of the cinematic medium, the camera, is the displacement of those visual conditions upon which, as a recording instrument, the camera is directly based. A wise man has said: "The camera does not lie." Why should it? Its truths are illimitable. Like all man's instruments, it is made to serve him in every potential fiber of its being. First, the camera displaced color by making it implicit in pictorial values, and then, in restoring it, provided a color gamut not that of either life or painting. But it displaced something more subtle than color; even more radically, it displaced that complacence which men had in subconsciously saying of a photograph, "It is very lifelike. Thank heaven it does not move!"—and the movie came as just as great a shock to those who secretly yearned to say, ". . . and look, it moves too!" Galatea moved, and answered Pygmalion's prayer, but in terms of pure movement, these having become a problem as soon as Galatea lived, Pygmalion's desire was an invitation to a greater catastrophe than perpetual and absolute inertia.

The movies alienated photography from painting by placing within it movement. This was so radical a challenge to reality that reality became a rival! After the novelty of the fantastic effects of the French pioneer, Méliès, wore off, it was plain that the conquest of "reality" remained. The illusion of normally clear vision and, above all, of dimension, had to be created in the artificial eye. By embracing movement, the still camera had initiated a new and different movement. The first law to be satisfied was not dimension, however, but the general articulation of the image: value and line. Méliès, of course, emphasized curiously the issue of dimension in his *Trip to the Moon*, yet at that time both the still and the moving cameras had much distance to advance toward the technical perfection of the single moment of vision.

Even as late as 1925 (I am thinking specifically of *The Big Parade*), the illusion of normal pace in movement had not been created—nor, for that matter, had the distribution of values yet become easy to the eye. In order to get enough *light* into the picture, that is, in order to see the delineation of the image well enough, the pattern had to be broken up too much. Lines were too sharp in distinction to the modulation of masses—the same effect which in the still photograph of that time had provided the same virtue without the eye being overtaxed. Thus, an extra effort to see came into being over and above the mental and visual concentration necessary for so variegated a spectacle as the movie. It was a long time before anyone connected with the industry understood how to solve the problem of pace, of having the actor move so as to create an *illusion* of normal action, and by that time, the camera itself was improving so much that only a subtle remodulation was necessary. Movies were then photographed—and run off—at completely arbitrary paces, creating unhappily unintentional effects.

Depth in intimate scenes—that is, of scenes in ordinary rooms—was difficult to achieve and was solved in one way by using over-sized sets, there being no effort to preserve the illusion of a normal-sized room. This dual *mode de convénance* and artifice to create depth have a curious echo in the contemporary cinema musical which sometimes, in depicting a theater stage within a movie, employs effects which could not possibly exist on any stage mechanism in use in the contemporary theater. *Only the mobility of the camera makes such effects possible.* Everything connected with the moving photograph eventually had to move in its peculiar manner, and assume a specific rôle in the whole mechanism of movie-making. When sound came, it was poor since, at first, the microphone remained stationary and since reproduction was not perfected. When the microphone moved with the same ease as the camera, sound became both "natural" and adequate to the effect desired. Hence the history of cinema technique involves perpetual displacements and replacements; transparent and egregious artifices have inevitably given way to concealed or "nonchalant" ones. In one sense, while the mechanism has become more complicated, the effects have become simpler, more "natural" and direct, and, though greater in number, are complex only in proportion to the trivial content they sometimes bear. At one end of the scale is the spectacle, which is supreme today as the musical comedy; at the other, is the cinema trick—the bravura offering of the keyhole type of exploitation, and by "keyhole" I mean merely the concentration on detail.

Even as actors on the stage, movie actors had to use make-up "for seeing's sake." Historically, stage make-up means character, as in masks; that is, the distance between the actor and the spectator was a definite element in determining the character mask. Primarily, the mask had meant a disguise of the real which permanently joined it to convention and symbols. Inherent, however, in the magically alienating faculty of the movies was that movie make-up implied a gradual displacement of the traditional objective of the *means* of make-up. This was because the invention of the still camera signified men's scientific desire to see more clearly—a desire to isolate reality and look at it at leisure. Thus, implying realism in culture, it implied it in artistic media. By photographing a mask, the *artifice* of the mask was expressed in distinction to the *reality of the illusion*; that is to say, the means and the end fell apart on the cinema screen to reveal a new problem in the chess of vision. The whole body of reality had in various ways to be "made up," but only in order to be more itself, to bring it closer. Therefore, in creating a purely visual intimacy between actor and audience that never before had existed, the movie displaced all the established visual conventions of dramatic expression, especially so far as the actor's person went. The point was *not* that actors should express emotions with their faces, but rather the reverse, that they should express their faces with emotions—to prove they were real, not waxworks, faces. Because of the primitive crudity of lighting, the actor's mouth, for instance, tended to become two almost undifferentiated black lines.

Moreover, the first movies were *silent*. Reality and artistic convention alike were alienated from the human portrayal. It is chiefly the absence of Bernhardt's voice which makes a somewhat grotesque marvel of her anachronistic style when seen in the movies. Visible on her face, alas, is a rapt listening to her own voice. The positive absence of sound swept away an element of reality from all living and inert images, and revealed a fabulously alienated world of movements. We must not forget that normal people suddenly fixed on the moving image *the concentration of the deaf.* Not only was written dialogue and narrative in the form of captions soon deemed necessary to the photograph when it moved and told a story, but the spectator began to feel need of a further device to create the artistic illusion of unity—the "whole of reality." This was music. Why music? Obviously, because it was auditory, but, more than that, because, being organized sound, music tended to contribute to the *totalized* effect of silent movement assisted by literature.

Still self-mindful, the movie camera produced clearer and more "seeable" photographs until all of a sudden —a thing which people had hardly noticed—a "surrealism" of make-up was brought to being: the black and white make-up, unlike the stage medium, seemed a disguise, an impediment to the reality of the effect. The presence of middle values, articulated grays, which had been relatively easy for the still camera, was suggested in cinema by the very fact that the actor's face, because it was painted, looked abnormally high-lighted: it looked *too* black and white because it is in the camera's nature as an instrument of accuracy to seek effects of realism. Even after a definite middle register had been reached, expressionist values in the foreign films exploited this very abnormal, black-and-white effect. In this medium, the cinema found its photographic science displaced by the abstract dimensional devices of painting. Modern painting, with its plastic conception of movement, had invaded the field of photography from which it was previously exiled. In the most extreme example of expressionist cinema, *The Cabinet of Dr. Caligari*, fantastic in content as well as in manner, the sets were painted structural designs conveying dynamic movement and a sense of space. But this was obviously a relative, by-the-wayside device, since in the movies it is the actually mobile means which are absolute, and hence there was no contribution to the genuine cinematic marvel through such means.

In early films, however, including all those made in America, the black-and-white effects were an absolute condition of the photography and spread through the total atmosphere of the movement without demarcation between static and mobile means of conveying movement. In total relationship, paradoxically, the object in relief tended to recede, that is, to draw together because of internally unarticulated value, in relation to the arbitrary black-and-white value, which came forward purely as a result of the camera lens and the reproductive medium. This was old-fashioned movie photography. At one time Cecil de Mille mimicked this quality in flat décors and costume, so that Gloria Swanson's face was merely the stylistic climax of the entire chiaroscuro. Nothing like an expressionist or *illusory* décor was used. Instead, it was a matter of the regular or realistic interior, "stepped up" in dramatic black and white, and sometimes almost caricatured. This was by no means altogether the accident of primitive studio lighting or unassisted exteriors (the "sunlight studio"). Two classical types of the simple, tendential black-and-white motif, shy of middle values, were the bathing-girl comedy and the Keystone-cop comedy, usually combined. The female figures against the sand of the beach, the black uniforms of the cops against every light value—this was the super-real vision of the early camera; namely, the *displace-ment* of mobile detail in respect to a totality of the single moving image. The sportive nature of the content, embellished by the flagrant designs of bathing-suit modes, assisted in this type of "dramatization" of cinema. Unforgettable also is Charlie Chaplin's silhouette against the broad glare of the road (he still uses it), as well as that fat eel, his mustache, frantically imprisoned in the fishbowl of his face.

"Beautiful" photography in 1944 is a platitude in every first-rate studio in Hollywood—I mean specifically photography freed from every condition limiting the total representational means with clarity as an end. Yet one kind of displacement occurred in Hollywood that is altogether characteristic of its middle period of inventiveness. When the camera began to show off its realism, its ability to catch action in all its detail as well as its sweep, the spectator was brought into the esthetic realm of physical effort and its illusory crisis of danger in a *more directly visual sense* than the stage could provide. This special effect was only gradually understood. From the beginning, Griffith, for instance, never ceased to expand the area of action (even if it meant placing a desk in the center of a large unoccupied area), desiring only to outdo the scope of the dramatic spectacle and yet to create its mobile details with some leisure. While as an artist remarkably intelligent, he failed to understand the natural possibilities of the camera, in that he assumed it was primarily extroversive, while it is equally introversive. He made many technical advances; the close-up, for example, as an accessory to the long shot, and vice versa. Working thus dialectically, this pioneering director added enormously to the dramatic vocabulary of the movies. But—dependent upon the visual psychology—there is more than one *kind* of narrative. While inferior to Griffith in ingenuity, Cecil de Mille, his successor, penetrated into the most primitive nature of the movie camera when he touched symbolically in his "bedroom dramas" upon the intimate genius of cinematic narration of images. He introduced bathroom sequences whose immodest whites exposed to the camera a secret place of light: a white mystery. In a wholly different way, Eisenstein, the Russian pioneer, realized *intimacy* with *montage*, which depends upon detail and stresses the fundamental imagery of the mind and its process of creating total thought by using objects as parts of thoughts * . . . Thus, as a generality, the

* Notice the discrete relation to *charade*; here the object, rather than its user, conveys the idea.

cinematic use of detail creates the subjectivity of mental states in narrative; namely, *psychology.*

Yet, of course, unless the content is dreamlike, the
total effect of cinema cannot be psychological in type.
In the previous chapter, I stressed those forces in
Hollywood working positively against that unity of
effect sometimes obtained even in a second- or third-
rate work of literature. Hence, when I refer to "total
effects" or suggest them, I am necessarily limited to
speaking of technique only. If there be no primary
unity—this very rarely occurs in American pictures,
much more often in foreign pictures—there is incom-
plete receptiveness in the spectator toward the events
on the screen as they aim at a total esthetic effect.
Hence, especially if one is sensitive, he resists many
aspects of the movies and automatically displaces them
in the total (or "charade") scheme of cinema values.
What is left then?

Always with us must be the positive accidents oc-
curring as results of this curious struggle between
forces, which we, as unusually passive spectators, reflect automatically rather than consciously. Consequently a displacement occurs *in us* corresponding to
the first displacement within normal vision when the
photograph appeared. I would call this an almost magical, perhaps a "surrealist," displacement of taste and
accustomed finality of judgment—a ritual which begins
with the sound of our change sliding down to us from

the change machine at the box office. Observe that the most potent contribution of the movie camera, which is its intimate genius in recording physical action, is quite capable of isolating itself. Scenes of great and intense action, with which Hollywood movies especially have been filled, grip us most when we are involved with their intimacy, their *visual selfness*, wherein we are the miraculously protected participants through unique courtesy of the camera. This does not mean that we measure our enjoyment by equating the effect of the physical mode with that of the spiritual and emotional mode! Alas, no.

Having solved so many problems of portraying action, Hollywood technicians employ the camera's genius for sheerly pyrotechnical ends; thus, the beauty of the camera may seem most eloquent just when its material is most incongruous and trivial. In its apparently scientific function of analyzing movement (*vide* the super-speed camera and its revelations) and of bringing us into closer visual proximity with the physical world than the eye is normally capable of achieving, the Hollywood camera is capable of introducing us *into* and then *out of* an imaginative idea with the utmost arbitrariness of timing, and with a purely bravura energy. So the camera seems to possess the wildness, the compulsiveness, and the interior meaning of the most instinctive life, such as that symptomatic in dreams, romantic poetry, and surrealist art.

When we go over a cliff in an automobile without being in it and see a gun being fired at us without being hit by the bullet (things which we imagine by a simple transposition of spatial points), the camera's eloquence automatically is alienated from the content of the movie and becomes a more or less independent effect. Yet because the causation is evident and simple, such thrills seem as perpetually amusing as discovering how the rabbit may appear from the empty hat. The most moving effect can be derived from such an episode as one recently in *A Woman's Face*, a chase on horse sleigh through snowy mountain trails. This beautifully and dynamically photographed sequence, because its given human motives were of almost no interest, can be filled with almost any content involving human terror, and in this situation the most available content is that of dreams, half-remembered associations of our past, or subconscious or conscious literary memories. The fact that we are so physically relaxed in our theater seats corresponds to our effort to woo the visual blank of sleep, and hence our eyes are peculiarly prepared for the unexpected and the overwhelming.

Like its first imaginative efforts on the part of Méliès and others, and like the extreme literary sophistication of Cocteau's *The Blood of a Poet*, the protean personality of the movie camera is romantic and of an unpredictable and shocking entrance. It catches us like guilty or timid children in an unguarded moment. Even in certain French, German, and Russian films of high artistic quality, it is evident that, in order to create the illusion of artistic unity, to keep the literary conception foremost, either fullness or depth of feeling on the one hand, or the cinematic possibilities of narrative exploitation on the other, have had to be slighted. The movie camera is unbelievably hospitable, delightfully hospitable—but supremely conceited. The spectator must be a suave and wary guest, one educated in a profound, naïve-sophisticated conspiracy *to see as much as he can take away with him.*

CHAPTER III

THE TECHNICOLOR OF LOVE

1. *The Background: The Theme*

A PALE, rational, dead-gray, blushlessly journalistic problem of the movies has been whether the act of fornication did or did not take place. Whenever this much-shunted problem appears, it is but an indication that the true importance of the sexual act and its biological secrets is being underrated. The conventional nature of theatrical representation, its ambiguity in regard to this alternative of *did* or *did not*, has consistently been exploited by the movie city as propaganda to get us to believe in the honor of hero and heroine. Although they may have been tempted and often deliberately or, so to speak, despite themselves, gotten into a sexually compromising situation, they have usually proclaimed their innocence implicitly or explicitly if only in their behavior toward each other the morning after. No stratum, section, or individual in society is disposed to deny the presence of carnal temptation—the impulse to give way to the purely animal feelings as they take by storm the male and female, but the morality of Hollywood ordains that, either to the scrupulous scientific eye or the givers-of-the-benefit-of-the-doubt, the hero and heroine, though they may suffer the consequences of an overt indiscretion, covertly obey "the law of sexual decency."

It is a little strange to reflect on the intelligence behind the etiquette which, barring evidence to the contrary, assumes the innocence of a particular man and a particular woman because general sympathy is presumed to be with them. A platitude is that any hero and heroine are the Chosen Pair . . . but in the profounder reaches of the human understanding and the art it produces, the Chosen Pair are almost of necessity the sinners, Adam and Eve. The relation of morality to carnal desire is an inescapable subject of imaginative literature, but this relation in all first-class novels and dramas is necessarily explicit concerning the physical relations between men and women. Such art (and one may list the better foreign movies) has at hand perfectly lucid devices for communicating this necessary information—call it "sex for the sophisticated" if you like. On the other hand, my own point of view may be accused of lack of sophistication. Is it not very possible that the "liberated," the cultured, or the merely cynical are one in thinking of the ambiguous shutting of a door, a fadeout on a kiss, and a fadein on the next morning: "But of course they went to bed together, it's obvious enough!" Yet in exactly what sense, I counter, if they did so? Suppose that only *thinking* made it so for the lovers? There would be a tremendous difference in the moral implications—a difference which, it may be observed, Hollywood ignores.

Look at the actual plots of any number of comedies, serio-comedies, and dramas involving such "sexual" situations as spending-the-night-in-adjoining-rooms. The crux of the situation is not whether they actually did or not, but whether others know they were in the situation and are thus in a position to draw their own conclusions; and also, on a third remove, whether those who know of the compromising situation care whether others (perhaps the whole community) know. Under the last circumstance, the would-be lovers usually are concerned with establishing their innocence, and indeed, it is this purely formal concern with "decent" appearances which the public would seem to require and for which it is properly appreciative. I say "the public," but I have already credited a large proportion of it with a cynical attitude toward this point *as a problem.* But is this attitude not a violation of the etiquette not only of that good will which one has for cinema personages (because one can sympathize with the genuine feelings of alarm about "appearances" no less than the rigors of temptation resisted or yielded to) but also a violation of the "etiquette" of art? For if we assume as true actions the ambiguity of which forms an element in the scheme of the story before us, we are willfully participating in its creation, wresting it from its makers, and molding it, at least in this all-important detail, to suit our own desires. This "anti-artistic" habit is not without a subtle retribution!

Let us look a little more closely at the precise manner in which action is communicated with regard to sexual behavior in Hollywood movie romances. Is it not true that, where there is unsatisfactory *post-facie* evidence that carnal union *did* take place, the actors and actresses nevertheless behave as though, to all ostensible appearances, *the temptation is mathematically equal to the surrender?* I remember Valentino's kidnaping of the heroine in his outstanding rôle of *The Sheik.* The woman (played by Agnes Ayres) resists his advances before the eyes of the audience. But are we to assume that such a man as this desert lover would be content, once he was so much aroused, with the mere ceremonial gestures of wooing? Passion does not always play the gentleman, even in a desert aristocrat. What of the long, nocturnal hours which are not shown and which breed their own monstrous etiquette? Again we see Miss Ayres as the trapped English beauty repulse her admirer. But may this not be because she has already been dishonored—or worse,

because she really wants to yield and has already suc-
cumbed in her imagination? Moreover, she knows very
well that she will be considered an object of mingled
pity and disgust, once she returns, if she ever does, to
her own society. Toward the end of the movie, did
Miss Ayres claim that her honor was unstained by the
desert chevalier? I forget. But it is possible to assume
that, under the circumstance that she was to "marry
the man," she believed a lie of this sort was justified.

In any case, cinema discretion placed a dusky hand-
maiden at Miss Ayres' elbow, apparently as her guardian angel, throughout her first night spent on the
brocaded divan of the Sheik's tent. But such a trans-
parently fictitious device did not disguise the psychology which operated here and hereafter in a thousand other cinema products from Hollywood. This is
an unconscious law of civilized psychology in the
United States, and is to the effect that if, though it
may be through no fault of their own, a man and
woman spend the night together in unsupervised privacy, and they are "normal" and roughly equivalent
in sexual attractiveness, they are bound to cohabit.
This is virtually an unspoken moral code, being, it is
assumed, only what the animal nature of the sexes
ordains, and hence any mortals so unfortunate or in-
discreet as to be together under such circumstances
have to stand the consequences. Indeed, it would be
insulting to assume they are not guilty, unless their

known probity and their word declares them innocent. This is a heritage of New England puritanism no less than of the feudal South, and is founded on the assumption that "morality" is largely a *negative, self-sacrificing* force . . .

Especially does the contemporary movie tend (as I have occasion to point out elsewhere) to displace seriousness in its perfection of the talkie and replace it with entertainment—even in regard sometimes to serious dramas and "tragedies." I have introduced the subject of morality only in order to provide a basis for discussing *what happens* in the movies. In recent examples, it is customary, when a "serious" style is desired, to have him, incidentally, marry the girl. This satisfies those movie-goers who, once the serious is essayed, must have it all official, legal. Consequently as a convention, the cinematic esthetic-serious in sex must be sanctioned by the facts and not by a speculative ambiguity. To be thoroughly true, up to the hilt, sex must have the permission of the legal guardian of morality. This is an *artifice*, mind you, and sometimes not especially noticeable; but, when it is not so noticeable, it is only because the original story depended, not so much on a positive conception of sexual morality, as on licentiousness as the frank form of its entertainment. Here is one of the most blazing of Hollywood hallucinations: the neglect of the fact that the Serious depends altogether upon comprehensiveness of morality and psychology, not only as to sex but everything else. The problem of factual ambiguity in sexual morality can never arise from citation of a *single instance*, because one generalizes from a single instance only with great danger to truth. The ambiguity inherent in They Did or They Didn't once is infantile and ludicrous among ambiguous situations; it tells little or nothing of character as a permanent aspect. Such an ambiguity is far too much in the past and is important only in analyzing the cases of sexual neurasthenics. From the viewpoint of morality, the only serious question is: The Same Two Do or The Same Two Don't—only with each other or also with others . . . indefinitely. And this would be merely the statistical aspect of sexual morality, necessary, however, to that psychological judgment which is part of all personal moralities. But, even from the serious viewpoint, morality is not *all*—and this is the strength of Hollywood: the metaphoric tendency of its myths, the chief of which is the Desert Island for two; that is why lovers are always being, semi-accidentally or accidentally, marooned. To the question, "What would you do if you were cast on a desert island with a beautiful blonde (or brunette)?" there is but one "conventional" answer. In a recent movie, *Bahama Passage*, Sterling Hayden was very slow in giving this answer, but, since it was the point of this particular

charade ("See Eve, see apple, see Eve eat apple . . ."),
he gave it.

Thus, under the head of the Romantic rather than
the Serious, there arises with or without hindrance in
the mythological world of the movies the dilating
Single Instance—the very pre-marital or post-marital
incident of fornication or adultery or near-same which
is involved in so many Hollywood comedy dramas
and society romances. The most frequent pattern, of
course, is that of Will He Ever Get the Girl, or Will
She Ever Get the Boy?—depending on which sexual
party is a little obtuse or a little timid. In basic terms,
the whole upshot of many such films is: Will the
Single Instance ever take place? Will Eve ever eat the
apple? After the climax (and of course a little pointed
isolation of the pair accomplishes this trick)—oblivion
—a blackout of the future . . . but the Single Instance
ad infinitum after the last reel (one hopes) . . .

How many times have I stayed to the end of a
movie plot, in simple-minded avidity, to be sure the
potential union took place at least once! Thus, the
hypnotic power of what is perhaps Hollywood's most
historic and sure-fire device. Although, radically speaking, either marriage, adultery, or fornication amounts
to a Symbol of Possibility more than a Tried Experiment or Old Habit, the more realistic and sophisticated movie products (usually straight from Broadway) convert the "possibility," when the plot requires

it, into a *dubious* habit, or else a boring kind of monotony, an almost static form of experience. Indeed,
marriage itself appears as the consequence of a glamorous misstep, and the only consequence of such a
consequence would be another glamorous misstep—
such as an infidelity. *When Ladies Meet* and *The
Women* are two excellent examples displaying this
logic.

The wife played by Greer Garson in *When Ladies
Meet* is a saddened but faithful sexual soul who at last
revolts against her husband's constant outside affairs
when she is introduced to the viewpoint (literally, face-
to-face) of one of his prospective mistresses. Miss
Garson, one of Hollywood's most intelligent actresses,
makes the rôle more credible and sympathetic than it
otherwise would have been. Hitherto, this lady has
taken the rather inverted attitude that her husband,
every time he returns to her contrite, has been unfaith-
ful once more to the institution of adultery! This time,
however, the "other woman" is so fine a girl and possesses such proud illusions that the wife feels she is
wrong to keep taking her husband back, and decides
to relinquish him to someone who may have a better
chance of making a successful marriage than she had.
The nobility of her impulse is obvious, but will it
stand a complete analysis? It seems more plausible to
suppose that she sees vividly in the pristine eagerness
of the other woman the foreshadowing of a pleasure

which is now a *historical matter* with her—an ideal, perfected moment of happiness which was lost in her marriage. May not the bitterness of her regret for this failure (due, possibly, to an irresponsible yielding to passion which the couple thought best to legalize) cause her to seek revenge against her sex? She may easily wish to expose other women to the probability of this denouement, since she may see repeated in the "forced marriage" aspect of the situation (created by her leaving him "free to marry") merely the reflection of her own experience. Hence, here is the Morality of the Single Instance! Supposedly, that is, in theory, a moral form continuously binding male and female, marriage is revealed by such psychology as the Romance of the Single Instance, an apotheosis of the first time the two indulged their carnal passion together. What is the explanation of such a mythical psychology but an overemphasis placed on the First Time—a sort of shock, a persistent sub-flowering of shame and guilt? The basic pattern is clear enough: marriage is not a complex spiritual and physical union to be revitalized by all manner of devices, and sustained by culture and imagination. It is, rather, a series of repetitions of an originally legalized sin; it is a compulsory, monolithic act of nature that one has received legal permission to repeat indefinitely. Alas, it was thus almost inevitable for Miss Garson as the married lady to conclude that an interesting *ambiguity*

flowed from that original They Did . . . Did They
really? This proves that the original act, in the moral
sense, must be divided into physical act and emotional
act; thus, *act* and *conception of act.* If the attitude of
the performers toward the *fait accompli* is not creative, protean, certainly nothing truly happy, nothing
to compare with the first moment, will come of it.

In *The Women,* too, with all its wisecracks, marriage is a patently monotonous, if sometimes inno-
cently parturitive, perspective on a historic act (done,
no doubt, with "mirrors" of time). This movie is primarily about the Legal Possessors of Male Property
and those who would deprive them of same by sexual
banditry. *Love* is conceived materialistically in terms
of mutually possessed property: the home, children,
and community reputation, as well as husband himself. It must not be forgotten that the husband is not
only a symbol but, under the present system, often
the sole material provider and maintainer of the wife
and her material environment. Does not the ambiguity
here lie in the fact that such wives as the main character in this movie are unequipped, esthetically or
materially, to be providers in case support is withdrawn
after marriage? Perhaps there is sexual fetishism in
her, even an approximation of what is known as
"love," but given the whole *ambiance* in *The Women,*
it would be very rash to romanticize beyond what is
actually revealed. Per se, it is a social, legal, and rather

crassly logical affair. True, the wife is obviously dissatisfied that the male property is being lost, yet it is she who insists on the divorce. Now what is divorce, historically considered? It is not merely a legal operation designed to protect the female and her children; it also constitutes a formal negation of those first moments of sexual happiness—the same moments turned, so to speak, inside out in public; it is public repentance for a "mistake." If it were not more than a pure economic arrangement, it would bear no such feared onus as it still does. Also, divorce leaves the ex-husband free to marry the wife's supplanter. The forces causing a wife to seek a divorce in the face of the necessary upheaval and against her husband's desire (this is his first infidelity) are no doubt roundly "practical." But in bedroom terms, an infidelity means but one thing: the woman does not give satisfaction. Now a public infidelity, such as it is in *The Women*, is an official exposure of this fact; namely, what is news to the public is not necessarily news to the wife . . . *unless* she has been under the naïve illusion that she still does give satisfaction. If she is not under such an illusion, she has had but one thing to console herself with: a historic incident, her marriage night, or her honeymoon. Again we meet, perforce, the desire of the losing woman to visit the same risk, and possibly the same fate, on her victorious rival. The generic problem of all such dramas reduces itself to the tendency of the male and female in wedlock to fail in converting the sexual act into a true *matrix* of pleasure, into the production of *children of desire*, who are at once actual progeny and progeny of the imagination.

In all this, of course, Hollywood slavishly imitates the coarseness and superficiality of the Broadway drama, and necessarily, I maintain, strives to outdo Broadway in all the fundamental artifices of sentimentality. The further away Hollywood gets from the reality and complexity of human problems, the closer it draws to the "single instance," not only of vision, but of morality. I think at once of the exquisite tones of Linda Darnell's skin in the most recent version of *Blood and Sand* with Tyrone Power. Since all art is but science of convention, the movies, beginning, as I discussed in the preceding chapter, with a startling mirror imitation of reality, relied (unlike the theater) on vision alone and by pure illusion; for the actors were not there, only their images were. As these images improved in quality and the visual illusion therefore was adequate, the movies competed with the stage, and finally, on the sheer basis of production, including multiple manufacture, overcame the popularity of the stage. Then movies acquired the voice of the stage and sound effects of an unrivaled reality; finally, and lastly in the sense of fulfilling the possibilities, technicolor came into being: a method of color reproduction which encompasses the palette and which, if it lacks the subtlety of painting, supplies in the colored moving photograph an artifice as varied as painting, insofar as it creates the illusion of visual reality.

At one time, color was a uniform tint, such as sepia (still used), or, rarely, tinted films of a very sloppy kind were exhibited. Rather irritating scenic short subjects of a blue-and-red prism came to be common, and were real for the paradoxical reason that they reproduced the dazzling effect of too much sunlight on the retina! Such devices are associated with the old plodding days of the films, when they indulged in the high jinks and low shadows of the mystery and Western serials. Then Griffith came with his pageantry and his forthright conception of the premarital single instances: rape or the marriage proposal. These were the poles of the screen's original technicolor of love. One was too plain for day, the other too plain for night. They were, like the bacchanals of which De Mille and Griffith were fond, crude conceptions, over-primitive, and either well-dated, or, as "real life," objectionable today. If they had been in color, and in such beautiful photography, would they have been acceptable even then? I imagine so, for a solemn moral attitude was taken (largely by way of a commentary which does not exist today: the subtitle) toward sexual excess, whereas today such excess is a form of entertainment, either in romantic comedy or fables of the Frankenstein genre. Primitive Hollywood was well aware that the most daring extremities can be reached under the cover of moral seriousness—a moral seriousness which, having been so thoroughly debunked in the last two decades, can seldom enter the scene of human entertainment today except in its most sentimental and innocuous forms. Both De Mille and Von Stroheim, though in differing genres, exploited the "sexual situation," especially with regard to adultery. They provided the "smart" dramas of their time, Von Stroheim going to bat for "freedom of sexual speech" and De Mille for some of the "naughtiness" that appeared now and again in Broadway farces or in such hell-raising among hicks as *The Squaw Man*. It is impossible to say how much such a relatively worldly man as Von Stroheim worked with tongue curled safely in his cheek so that it would not puncture his face. As Hollywood innovators, he and De Mille undoubtedly brought a moral seriousness about real-life problems and frankness about marital relations to a new high for the movie city. But this contemporary fact must be faced: sex is no longer a *subject*; indeed, it has been taken over in the large sense by the psychoanalysts. So that there was really no struggle when Hollywood romance set out to subdue Hollywood morality: it had always been the stronger force. Hence sexual morality (when it is not a comic myth as in *Don Juan*) is a matter of incidents and metaphors; of rape, isolated seductions, or courtship.

With the importation of Ernst Lubitsch, a new sophistication came to Hollywood with a brand of sex comedy European in flavor. Where Von Stroheim had been heavy-handed, Lubitsch could be delicate; where Von Stroheim had been bluntly moral, Lubitsch was subtly immoral. For Hollywood, it was a coming-of-Continental-age. It was the "normal" view of sex, situated between the exotic romance and the monster-of-rape shocker. In the following chapter I shall discuss a most important aspect of Hollywood's presentation of sex: the myth of the somnambules; but this is thoroughly exotic, a kind of "domesticated" primitiveness . . . like the image of herself in a cage drawn through the streets of Rome which caused Cleopatra to prefer death. The modern Queens of Love among actresses do not flinch, however, at a parallel fate!

Beyond, beneath, among, and—indeed—saturated with all the more mythical forms of sex, American movies maintain a certain necessary constant—a constant as indispensable as good photography and articulate speech. It is almost equivalent to a grammar of sex as opposed to its metaphors, its large myths. It is a form of etiquette practiced by ladies and gentlemen of fiction, aided and abetted by actors and actresses of Hollywood. For the purposes of this chapter, I call it the Technicolor of Love.

2. *The Foreground: The Incident*

The technicolor screen has form, color, and sound
—all the actual perquisites of Vivian Leigh and Leslie
Howard, Olivia de Havilland and Clark Gable. Considering that *Gone with the Wind*, as a work of literature, is at best but a uniquely elaborate scenario, a
third-rate novel, these actors and actresses are material
improvements upon their fictional prototypes. As Scarlett O'Hara, Rhett Butler, Ashley Wilkes, and Melanie
Hamilton, they impersonated a long and esteemed
line of Hollywood "types." The preparation of Mar-
garet Mitchell's ready-made epic, which as usual
started with the first gun from the arsenal of the press
agent, was itself a drama. The producers unerringly
realized that the picturization of a novel which had
populated the country with prostrate and unwinking
readers was only to be done without stint of money or
veneration. Vivian Leigh was finally chosen, not only
for her talent and because she suited the part physically, but because the producers, having signed her
last among the four featured players, had decided they
must save on expenditure after putting out so heavily
for the other three, especially for the messrs. A canny
choice, for, though the war was responsible for calling
Miss Leigh from these shores, she won the statuette
for the year's best screen performance, as well as her
first rôle in an American film.

Scarlett was so instantly appreciated by hordes of literate women because she reflected a typical (or at least typically envied) lack of moral rectitude and was what might be called a "strong-minded" sexual type. She was temperamental and sensual. While eliminating certain coarser suggestions about the character as created in the novel, Miss Leigh succeeded in communicating the waywardness, the grit, the depth of instinct, and the flavor of "bitchiness" which Miss Mitchell's second-rate wisdom so carefully pinned to so many of her many pages. She also succeeded in being "naturally" attractive, like a highly intelligent advertisement for unpretentious make-up. It was her triumph as a performer, moreover, that she carried with her an essential: obvious femaleness. I have often reflected that one of the least fortunate traits of Hollywood is its temporal conventions; there is little chance among all its technical blandishments for character development in the running-off time of a movie. Consequently we can reflect that concentration on dramatic turning-points of sexual conduct, regardless of their moral truthfulness, has been obligatory on account of the *length* plus the *treatment* of a Hollywood movie. But the sheer length of *Gone with the Wind* offered some semblance of the seriousness of pace which dominates the best European films. *Gone with the Wind* communicates a sense of character duration —the sense of people existing within time and society as in a single and unremitting milieu. One of the gravest Hollywood faults is that the passing of time is too conventionalized—too much a temporal gap bridged by cheap montage effects (calendars peeling off their numerals, and so on). A sense of both change and progression is supplanted by non-plot elements, rigid symbols, and external events such as the seasons—usually because somebody in a movie is always patiently waiting for the plot to catch up with his desires or else lagging behind nature. This has been curiously stressed by sagas of time in which actors and actresses are seen from childhood or youth to old age. With make-up at its peak, it affords a wonderful opportunity for clever thespians to prolong their acting careers. But vegetable decay is a very weak (if ostentatious) substitute for drama. Here again we have the pedantic nature of Hollywood exploiting the vocabulary of make-up and the ingenuity of its lighting department.

A narrative with the scope and leisure of *Gone with the Wind*, however, could accommodate many of the screen's favorite vanities without noticeable injury: its picturesque episodes, its action sequences, its technicolor opportunities, and its bathroom-mirror fixation upon the faces and motions of the leading players. The scenic sweep and variety of visual pattern, rightly considered appropriate to this movie, necessitated some repetition of the feeling of Griffith's camera: the obligation to keep at a certain respectful distance from the players—a convention which makes the close-up more dramatic by a switch to touching distance, sometimes without much notice, and its consequent hint of indelicacy. It is well known that the movie camera tends to make life seem larger than it is. This is the larger-than-lifeness that means most to the Moment of Love. It should not amaze that I refer to the manners, pertinent or "impertinent," of the camera, by no means so impersonal as some still imagine it to be. The camera would be impersonal only if it were unselective—if it were allowed to report "all that goes on," although this omnipresent eye is either a Utopian dream or a pure (and empirically dubious) convention.

Basic narrative is the notion of what happens in the physical sense. Soundless cinema was much more "basic" in this respect, less sophisticated in the showmanship sense—a fact which provides another reason for the greater seriousness of pre-sound cinema. Letting the pantomime of nature "speak for itself," with a limited number of verbal captions, entailed a more rigid visual logic than that of sound cinema, which reverts to the static background of the stage maintained in the eye while the actors are speaking. Thus, adding the voice to the movements of the actor resulted in a limitation where there had been a freedom. But this also made the psychology of the movie more akin to the novel, for when a shift of scene was de-

sired, it could be done just as in the novel, and yet
without loss of the auditory; namely, dialogue had a
more strategic position in the new technical medium
than it had had in silent days.

Yet what happened? Naturally, the screen was slow
in acquiring good dialogue or a shrewd placement of
dialogue in the whole scheme of cinema. If we glance
(not so irrelevantly as may be at first supposed) at
the novels of Henry James, we notice that a complicated social etiquette infuses the relations between
the sexes, an etiquette expressed both in terms of psychology and conversation. We notice that this novelist
apparently placed no value whatever upon what actually occurred, or might occur, in the bedroom, and
thus is much closer to Hollywood than one might have
supposed. Indeed, in James' novels, dialogue is the
"natural" medium of sexual intercourse—verbal rather
than carnal conversation. It happens that, without
having at all the conscious moral purpose of James,
Hollywood assumes that a manipulation of dialogue
in relation to indicated psychology is a sufficient convention to convey sexual reality. Note that this is a
convention for strict purposes of communication, and
is not what Hollywood depends on for conveying its
ultimate presentation of life; for this, it depends on
the moving photograph, preferably colored. At the
same time, it does not hesitate to utilize what might

be called the "Jamesian" device of the voices of people in love, transposing them to the audible oral medium . . .

In the plays of Bernard Shaw and others, no less than in the novels of Henry James, speech is a specific form of love-making and a powerful element in creating sexual situations. Shaw specifically isolated this theme in *Pygmalion*. Thus, in novels and plays, both more speechified if diversely so than the movies, the voice, vehicle of words, is a purely esthetic weapon in the hands of the artist, both as to literary inventiveness and the assumed charm of the actor's linguistic style. Shaw's professor in *Pygmalion* was played by Leslie Howard, a coincidence meaningful to the present theme. The Galatea tutored into cultural life by Pygmalion was ostensibly merely an instrument intended by Shaw, as a satirist, to embarrass the British society of his time, but she was also a symbol of sly propaganda for conversation as a builder of love. What is the denouement? Mr. Howard's professor is hardly aware that the flame of love has awakened in the breast of the linguistic phoenix he has created, and she has to bring to his attention the very motive, love, by which his prototype, the legendary Pygmalion, was actuated! Hollywood is just as forgetful as this professor and just as concerned as his pupil. It has made use of the voice mostly for purposes of snobbery. Naturally, if the spoken word was to invade the Holly-

wood studio, it had to be by way of the most dulcet
vocalists and the best elocutionists. These inevitably
came from the stage, dominated of course by the British accent. All actors in the movie city got "instruc-
tion" purely as a matter of utilitarian strategy. They
had to be understood; the words, whatever they were
or portended, had to be communicated. It has been
only by a sort of inadvertence that the voice, as a
builder of love, as an esthetic instrument of the sexual
emotion, has been given a place in the talkies. Hollywood's psychology of love is that an anterior fact of
mutual magnetic attraction exists and this rigid, quasi-
bedroom fact results in the act of wooing, regarded in
essence as a *legal convention* rather than an eloquent
ceremony. Thus it was merely unavoidable that attached to the word spoken by the voice of a British
actor was the Lady and Gentleman and their natural
bodies as dressed animals.

I introduce such an apparently salacious idea on the
grounds that clothes have a symbolic importance equal
to that of voice in sexual relations. The difference between a man and a gentleman, for instance, is that the
latter wears his clothes as though he were born in
them and they grew with his body; the man is within
the gentleman even as the woman within the lady.
But in the act of divesting, just as in the act of ceasing
to speak, lies a great morality. It is a ritual because
secrets will be learned, and it is the pure depth of such

secrets as well as their dimensions and form that satisfy the seeker. Beneath all, and enclosing it like an envelope, is the necessity for evaluating what occurs in the single instance of organic sex—but this evaluation can be gained only by understanding it in relation to a total society of acts and thoughts, acts and imagined acts. As it happens in Gone with the Wind, the heroine, so vitally inspirited with sex, has no such means, and never, despite her cleverness, develops any, for arriving at those decisions which would permit a secure and permanent sexual happiness.

Her golden experience, Ashley Wilkes, eludes her, and she accepts instead Rhett Butler, a charming rake, a "gentleman" gone a bit too cosmopolitan for provincial society. This is Scarlett's "revenge"; indeed, her entire life is a series of bittersweet alternatives slipped into envelopes of postponed solutions. Miss Mitchell in the novel is consistently clear about this. The mercurial nature of Scarlett's emotions is a wonder of monotony; fear, rage, malice, desire, despair—all that she requires to escape them is another moment of life, another tick of the clock. Scarlett is always naïvely imagining her experiences in the fractional terms of absolutes divided by mere conveniences, and (the psychology is perfect) this is the result of her bad and certain conscience; she knows that her hyperbolic emotional temperament does not hit bottom and never will. Yet she knows that nothing but death or crippling will lick her, and nothing does. Why? Because her mind is capable of infinite postponement in trying to recognize any final, unpleasant truth, any fixed, distasteful fact. The movie like the novel ends on this symphonic note after Rhett Butler has deserted her: "I'll think of it tomorrow, at Tara," she says. "I can stand it then. Tomorrow, I'll think of some way to get him back. After all, tomorrow is another day."

As a heroine, Scarlett is a masterpiece of self-deception, self-bribery: she can go on happily only because, in spite of her failure of character, life has bestowed on her a faculty of optimism, a faculty of isolating desire from its crisis in action—a faculty which makes her the screen's typical heroine of all time and a symbol of Hollywood itself. You might say it is through no fault of hers that Ashley Wilkes, in their crucial interview after his return from the battlefield, does not take her, as he says, "here in the mud like a —," and so precipitate a separate phase in her emotional life. For then, according to his code, he would have had to divorce Melanie and marry her. The trouble with such a morally indecisive heroine as Scarlett is that she contaminates her creator: the creative vision itself reaches a stalemate, which only Hollywood's technicolor of love can loosen and liberate.

In this era of civilization, it is an instinct of the woman to be pseudo-somnambulistic: to let the man decide . . . Is the tone of his voice not authoritative and beautifully registered to hint of stepping down from that authority and, out of loving mockery, playing the slave? Though Shaw himself insists that masculine hegemony ended with Victorianism, I think the relative quality of voice in the sexes proves my point. If the male is by no means so strong as he was, owing to the equalization of male and female in the economic world, the vestiges of his power remain in symbols and myths that survive in art and its representations. The best male voice of this kind belonged to Leslie Howard, I believe, and so it was only poetic that he should play Ashley Wilkes, abdicator from sexual action. Howard's closest competitors in Hollywood among the British were Laurence Olivier, Herbert Marshall, and Ronald Colman; among the foreigners, Charles Boyer. It is possible, I suppose, to prefer the last-named to Mr. Howard, but as far as the voice bred alone in the British bone goes, Mr. Marshall's is a trifle burry and obtrusively mannered. Moreover, physically, he hasn't Mr. Howard's qualifications, and if Mr. Olivier (now lost to Hollywood) is more personable than Mr. Howard, he has not so much finesse as an actor. Mr. Howard's effect was slenderness without fragility; he had a virile neck and youthful, wavy, golden hair—that it was, or was not, his own hardly matters. Where it is a case of the genteel male animal, any artifice or disarray of artifice becomes his own through moral domination of what is above the neck and inherent in the most articulate portion of anatomy, the face. It is that portion, rising with such promise from the contemporary male collar, and riding like a wave permanently suspended above an ocean, that concentrates in itself the communicated tenderness for which the female perpetually searches in the male. What is there may constitute a symbolic guarantee, not only of infinite generosity of all kinds, but against possible overestimation of any other part of his body. It is fear of this overestimation which the female must struggle against, as well as the overestimation itself, knowing as she does that man will unscrupulously hold this over her once he is morally weak enough to coldly exploit her, either as an instrument of pleasure or of economic support. This is the *other*, not the self, bribery of women. Seeking the complete conquest of the human body, not only in life, but as our eyes roam through endless feet of film, we are bound to encounter and attempt to judge man and woman without their clothes; to see them, that is, as the man thing and the woman thing. Johnny Weismuller, Buster Crabbe, Jon Hall, Errol Flynn, and Victor Mature are perhaps the most vivid among those men who have stripped without teasing; whereas the bodies of such women as Dorothy Lamour, Rita Hayworth, Betty Grable, and Paulette Goddard are stripped either for the dance floor or the boudoir quite as a routine part of civilized or semicivilized living in the movies.

As the somnambule (that is, as the apparently involuntary candidate for the sexual act), woman must advertise her latent strip-tease personality through excessive languor or excessive activity. But man, the gentleman, accomplishes the same thing by a golden mean, an ideal modulation of the clothing pelt and the naked body. While the same thing is theoretically true of women as ladies, American and English women are almost incapable of a female correspondence to this male achievement. European women are a different question, but even they, in American movies, are compelled, in order to "get their man," to enact the somnambule; namely, to resort to the unspoken *monosyllable* of dreamlike acquiescence. Curtain. Finis. You know what happens next.

Scarlett could have been happy if she had seen in Ashley's face *after the sexual act* all that she saw (or thought she saw) there before. Then she would have believed it, for it would have been a *verified* moral interpretation of the raptures of the flesh. Scarlett's perception to the bottom of the sexual dimension was perfectly clear, and therefore she was in a position subconsciously to acknowledge to herself woman's universal danger: male fetishism. As provincially limited a kind of culture as Ashley Wilkes represented, he was capable of providing Scarlett with the reassurance she desired: a promise against enslavement. On the contrary, Rhett Butler provoked her to this enslavement, to which she did not utterly yield, only because of her thwarted desire for Ashley. Mr. Gable was excellent for the part because his face held a purely sensual and limited promise. It is not that he could not also fulfill (as he did) the duties of a husband and father. It is a question of the logic of the male "strip tease," and thus of sexual style, and thus, finally, of erotic sensibility.

The natural and universal reticence of feminine etiquette under masculine hegemony makes her look for enlightenment first to the male face. However "emancipated" woman has become, only "professional" women of one sort or another go beyond certain bounds of purely sexual aggressiveness. When his eyes drop to her breasts, she is unconsciously dismayed, fearful, and the only thing that reassures her is his voice, a lyric instrument upon which her whole soul leans as though its harp strings were a staff. If it is the jungle, and thus the underside of sexual nature, which packs a punch in the body of Johnny Weismuller, et al., it is civilization, and thus the overside of sexual nature, which packs a punch in the voice of Leslie Howard, et al. The effect of the former is to knock the female senseless; the effect of the latter is to awaken her. Yet the body remains, in any case, and receives through the genius of Hollywood the gift of technicolor. Scarlett heard *seduction*, a technicolor of love, in Rhett's voice, whereas she heard *courtship*, another technicolor of love, in Ashley's voice. It is possible that Ashley Wilkes would never have satisfied Scarlett O'Hara. In the end, she decides she does not love him, but it is pretty transparent that this is because she has despaired of provoking in him enough animalism to "take her" simply and without benefit of clergy. But although the novelist, as the novel is only paper and ink, may have control over these matters, what control have the actor and actress, living images in the opening envelopes of technicolor? Even in flesh tones, technicolor does not reproduce the unity of colors seen directly in nature. Each color tends to remain jealously, arrogantly in its own patch, and though it may be harmonized with other colors by prearrangement, it cannot be married to its environment as color in nature. It is true that one color, such as fire-red, may deluge the screen (as it does in *Gone with the Wind*) but obviously this is a tour de force. Under normal circumstances, lip-red will return wilfully to its source, Miss Leigh's lips, or husband-pink will readily reseat itself on Mr. Howard's forehead. Thus, in technicolor, flesh color is subtly an individualized perquisite of the human body and flaunts its symbolic flags to give notice that it prevails in every recess of its natural domain.

When the artistic conception of a work of art does

not dominate and fulfill all that we know and expect from a work of art, its elements are invariably liberated into an anarchy, a free form of competition among themselves. It is into such an analogous world of dream that the movie liberates its components, the author of *Gone with the Wind* being in a parallel position with the Freudian "censor" of waking life. During sleep, this censor is evaded; likewise in the life of the imagination, objective reality, which poses as a censor of desires, is removed, and the mind lives among free images. As I have emphasized already, the movies entertain a very powerful conspiracy to dissuade the imaginative life from resorting to its own maneuvers, its own daydreams or artistic works, and to adopt instead the free, often perverse or irrelevant play of desires issuing from their works. So far as Hollywood goes, however, this function is in effect the antithesis to the effect produced by works of art, for the Hollywood pattern does not dominate or satisfy our esthetic instincts. Thus we, the spectators, are offered a collaborative rôle with the other Hollywood employees, and Scarlett O'Hara, who cannot unify or control her processes or be certain of an object of desire, is a true symbol of Hollywood itself and so superunited with her audience.

The single instance of sex is but a profoundly covert germ which, like the unified and adequate mental conception of a work of art, must flower into an overt and amplitudinous objectivity; that is, into a satisfying symbol of reality. Set within a cinema work of art, Scarlett and Ashley assume in their sexual situation an ominous isolation, which has made all the speculation set down here possible. The first domain of isolation (remember the desert island!) is that they are Leslie Howard and Vivian Leigh: namely, they have a unique capacity to please the spectator entirely without reference to their characters within the scheme of the movie. At the same time, their strategic position is that they are obeying the etiquette of acting, of artistic pretense. The peculiar qualifications of this actor and actress also make them *apt*; we pay tribute to the *casting*.

The emotion of not wanting a hero to die, of wanting a heroine to be happy, is an infantile one; the result of naïve identification of ourselves with personages of fiction that we possessed as children. When reading Dostoievsky or watching a performance of Shakespeare as adults, we consider this habit absurd, yet sitting in a movie theater we are continually caught up in the Hollywood conspiracy to do as well as possible for our favorite characters. Look at the situation: first of all, they are living people, and we realize that Camille does not really die, and that Scarlett O'Hara as anyone but herself (as for instance, Vivian Leigh) might have succeeded in provoking Ashley Wilkes as anyone but himself (as Leslie Howard, shall we say?)

to take her that day in the field at Tara. As we sit in this dilemma, the images before us are moving, the dialogue is relentlessly proceeding. We begin to face (and, since the theater is dim, why not?) all the facts of the particular qualifications which these two possess as Man and Woman and which I have been discussing. In our imagination, and initiated already into the classic dilemma of They Did or They Didn't, we begin to associate with these ideas, before we know it, the idea, They Might Have; psychologically, this is equivalent to They Did.

All the while, we are observing the actions on the screen, listening to the words, and hardly aware of our subconscious. Miss Mitchell clothes Ashley in "grotesque rags" on his return from the battlefront, but Mr. Howard wears merely a disheveled but very whole uniform of the Confederate Army, gray and gold, to match his hair. He has divested himself of his coat in the scene with Scarlett near the barn, but his trousers are merely rumpled and need no mending, his boots unimpaired. Hollywood will not yield its quantitative richness to realism! Scarlett wears a torn brocaded dress and an apron of sackcloth; a shabby shawl is around her shoulders, and a bright snood pathetically gathers up her hair. Here is the test of Ashley's gentlemanliness and Scarlett's weak womanliness, which is only the natural result, as he chivalrously acknowledges, of her courageous assumption of the masculine part at Tara after the catastrophes of the war. The situation is ideal for a breakdown of his resistance under the force of Scarlett's feminine pathos and desirability. They are both physically and morally weary, and the whole world, saving the earth at their feet, seems to have been snatched from them. The hypnotic effect of Mr. Howard's thoroughly civilized head in this scene is most conspicuous; assuredly, it is the chief contribution of British civilization to society and somehow still alive. That artful tact of the male, which Hollywood, with all the heroism of Emily Post, has imitated in its scripts for the purpose of polite scenes between the sexes, was triumphantly illustrated by Mr. Howard's complete vocal and anatomical wardrobe. As a result, the latter became a true symbol of that sexual tact which Ashley (being married to Melanie) was supposed to be applying to Scarlett, for whom he felt a sharp animal desire. Scarlett's clothes and his become the naked suits of human animals in love at this stage of civilization. Of course, Ashley is painted as an idealistic, almost bookish male in love with a serene, leisurely, and dreamlike, aristocratic mode of life. But this only points his obvious Hollywood avoirdupois. Scarlett says of her sisters and the sick Melanie: "I could leave them . . . I'm sick of them . . . tired of them . . ." Later, struck with quick sympathy, he "came to her swiftly and in a moment had her in his arms, cradling her comfortingly, pressing her black head to his heart, whispering: 'Dear! My brave dear, don't! You mustn't cry!' " On the screen, his arms *do* "cradle her comfortingly." Surely, it is not that the rules of etiquette have been disobeyed. On the contrary, the visualization and vocalization here are as good as the scenario for them, and no doubt such personages as Miss Mitchell's characters existed at that period of the South. In fact, it is because Miss Leigh and Mr. Howard exist so snugly in this pattern, with such magnificent visual illusion, that we don't mind fitting in with them. But to submit to this pattern entirely would be to accept the *art* of the movies, whereas we know in the back of our heads that this is impossible. Leslie Howard and Vivien Leigh can never remain in our minds as Ashley Wilkes and Scarlett O'Hara. After all, we are to see them in other productions, other patterns. And because their personalities are powerful enough to gain them excellent rôles, they emerge from the artistic pattern of *Gone with the Wind* as the naked body from its clothes—they shine through their multiple masquerade as the sexual performer shines through his preliminary motions of courtship. The male voice is the spokesman for all those tongueless organs whose "speech" must be subordinated to the human personality as will and morality and is itself a fetish against the fetishism which is capable of dismantling the human organism and separating one part from another as in a debacle. The divestment for sex is a mock debacle, and if the mutual pairs of hands pluck and dislodge, it is only under the originally visible guarantee, by all the features of the face (above which golden hair is an angelic token), that clothes are but conventional illusions, and that the intention of the covered part is as open to the daylight and as subject to as much criticism as the uncovered part.

What a terrible danger does Tyrone Power in his unaccustomed rôle as the *Son of Fury* undergo in this respect! For to show the skin beneath the skin of the civilized animal is to paste rudely on the conventional urban eye an illusion of an ultimate dimension. But the true ultimate dimension is and must be morality— the infinite, rather than the single, instance: the evaluation in time and social experience rather than the evaluation in space and individual experience. And this is the romantic illusion: the absolute evaluation on the Single Instance, the finger pointing to the closed door, and the whisper: *They Do.* Sexual life cannot be only this. Yet only true art could *succeed* in perpetuating such an illusion; otherwise it is transient, a "mock wedding." Technicolor is but an attribute of art, a pure medium of representation. It is the latest, perhaps the final, contribution of Hollywood to that illusion of objective reality which has been its dilating destiny. The color of Miss Leigh's skin: it is not precisely the color of flesh. It is artifice. But behind all these incredibly transparent artifices, like so many useless dermal layers (pure because we know the living persons are not there—these are only their reflected images), is the ultimate fact of human life, human desires, human movements, human etiquette. Technicolor takes us to the ends of the earth, away from the costumes of Miss Leigh and Mr. Howard, and back again in an instant. Every visible and undefended part of them, flesh or fabric, is isolated, by dint of the transparent facts of illusion, from any organized resistance to our will of imagination. As the words go on, as the routine proceeds, as these human beings obey all the conventions of art, manners, and their sexual natures, as we know they have obeyed them in faithful and sincere mimicry (since their obedience is being mechanically reproduced for us), we are tempted to contradict it all, to unmake history, to stop the film at a certain point, and to direct the deployments of the remainder. Since there is no supreme artistic illusion to hinder us, the technicolor epidermis of the screen is ripped open . . .

CHAPTER IV

THE SOMNAMBULES

THE tradition of the somnambules in the movies is more conspicuous than those who put two and two together to make money may have noticed. It is only prudery, of course, that would prevent conceding the fact that the somnambule's myth essentially signifies the "ritual" readying of woman for sex by depriving her of her conscious powers through hypnotism. But she does not have to get up from her bed and walk in her sleep to respond to intangible influences of desire and fear. In ordinary, "waking" terms, somnambulism in women is susceptibility to seduction by psychological tour de force. *The Phantom of the Opera*, a silent movie, very well illustrated that the somnambule, acting under some strange power which defiled her, was a percolation of the Gothic romance into modern art. Although she has appeared from time to time, her success per se has never equalled that of the vampire, who, far from being unaware of her disreputable state, was not only acquainted with her wickedness but exulted in her erotic triumphs. I remember a Hollywood "Trilby" some fifteen years ago, as well as the heroines of old mystery thrillers, hypnotized and at the mercy of the villain's amorous brutality. Their state of danger was a logical antithesis to their conscious chastity—a sort of mock retribution with the devil as the instrument.

Three of the most famous vampires I remember are Theda Bara, Valeska Suratt, and Nita Naldi, though by the time Naldi arrived, the descriptive word was already well dated. Yet vampirish movements in women continued to be popularly—and justly—termed "snaky." No doubt, "The Serpent of Old Nile" had much to do with the verbal tradition, and indeed, more than one gaudily mature Cleopatra graced the native screen with a snake as both physical instructor and murderer. All the vampires fascinated their victims with the same paraphernalia of hypnotism as that with which Svengali subdued Trilby: a serpentine pantomime and a glittering eye, appurtenances of the most ancient magic. The somnambules, or the hypnotized ladies, were rendered almost rigid, or at least incapable of very articulate movement. This was precisely the effect produced in the unfortunate males who came within the enchanted zone of the vampire. We have to conclude that nature has provided a

poetical antinomy in the sexual struggle. Yet Hollywood—as was almost inevitable—did not allow this antinomy to remain static. What was not inevitable was
that the variation should have been as distinctive and
triumphant as that embodied by the Gish sisters, Mae
Marsh, and a few successors. Though physically frail,
these glamor girls of the sunlit sets possessed a virtue
that was strong. Of course, they too had a literary an-
cestry, but one more specialized and recent than that
of their vampirish sisters. Although, at first, they
seemed merely the delicate romantic heroine of decent
but rather humble birth, they were seen to exhibit
signs of the strong-mindedness of Jane Austen's heroines. Consequently they had a dialectic element which
militated against their serving the European convention of the female as born under the star of Venus,
and hence a "natural" sinner, not so morally responsible as the male. But D. W. Griffith, who may indeed
have been influenced by Barrie—who knows?—preferred to conceive woman as naturally virtuous—a kind
of Eve versus a Lilith conception, the latter realized
by the vampire. Yet this director had a somewhat Vic-
torian sensibility and modeled his famous heroines as
women less susceptible than Eve. Not only did Lillian
and Dorothy Gish refuse to consider the snake either as
a physical or moral instructor, but they would deny it
even their metaphysical toleration unless there were a
minister and his book in the background. Though,

later, Dorothy took over gamine rôles, the simple, if essential, condition of the typical Griffith movie was that the exquisite sense of chastity possessed by Lillian should be constantly threatened. The value of this pattern is obvious. What is remarkable is the special physical state that resulted in Miss Gish: *she became a permanent lyric of jumpiness.* It seems doubtless that Griffith trained her in her mannerisms as though she were a canary . . . I used to read of numberless rehearsals of one short scene, the very arduousness of which must have contributed to the effect Griffith desired in his star. His judgment was excellent, since Lillian became a human canary who, while her song was perforce unheard, portrayed her fright beautifully in the visible flutter of her body and arms. What a strange antithesis for the legendary somnambule! Before she became defenseless, and thus an object of desire to the subconscious minds of the male audience, the somnambule-type had had to be hypnotized and rendered utterly passive and obedient.

Surely both the anti-somnambulistic vampire and the pre-somnambulistic canary are discrete but complementary types, together forming a dual opposition to the orthodox somnambule, the woman who submits herself readily to the powers of sleep or hypnotism. Both vampire and canary illustrate the sexual excess of the female herself, while the somnambule is merely an instrument of the sexual excess of the male. This distinction, self-evident with the somnambule and the vampire, is superficially ambiguous with regard to the canary. Why is the canary not merely Consciously Frightened Virtue? Indeed, why should the canary not be coupled with the somnambule, since when awake and rational, they both resist unwelcome seduction? But the whole psychological hypothesis of the somnambulistic and hypnotized states here interferes with the argument, for this hypothesis implies a split in the desires of the woman. While, in her abnormal state, she *cannot* resist seduction, this does not necessarily presuppose that a level of desire does not exist in her which she may obey under certain conditions of release. Thus, the somnambule (and this is the basis on which I evaluate the Hollywood actresses in this chapter) is the *generic female* rather than an *individual female*.

In defining the canary, we have to assume that all women know, and understand more or less consciously, what does and does not excite the male. Unless a woman wishes to feign defenselessness for her own aggressive end of seduction by pretending to be asleep or drugged, she knows that *movement*, particularly if of an extremely feminine kind, informs the male perfectly of her various irresistible and lively charms; namely, the more active a frail woman is, the more effectively she displays her inviting fragility. Only when the female is impassive, therefore, can she presume to claim *neutrality* of her own emotion. To the snake figure of the vampire, we oppose the statuesque figure of the somnambule. Yet, while grace of the snake and grace of the canary are quite different, they are, as symbolic patterns for female deportment, to be considered equally conscious as part of the personality. If "clean competition" be the issue, the snake by no means has the advantage over the canary. And competition exists, even if it be only the professional competition of rival actresses.

I use such socially outdated symbols as "vampire" and "canary" for the sake of the historicity of my argument no less than for the sake of revealing the profound perspective of time in which I wish to situate the Hollywood somnambules. Throughout this book, I have tried to deal as much as possible with basic psychology and basic norms. From a scientifically analytical viewpoint, the motions of fear closely resemble those of strong desire when the emotion is unrepressed. The peculiarly artificial style of Miss Gish's femininity (I speak of her Griffith days only) must be considered a synthesis of fear and desire: *fear* in the sense of timidity and virginal propriety, and *desire* in the sense of flirtation, an impulse to be noticed by and to please the male. These counter emotions produced their refined hieroglyph of the Gish femininity under the Svengalism of Griffith, who conceived Miss Gish as a Trilby in whom pantomime was substituted for voice. It is worth noting here that both Trilby and Lillian are making love under the direction of their masters, and, moreover, making love *professionally*, one as a songstress, the other as a movie actress. Consequently the element of evil in the hypnotic males involved is forced to give way to a more or less impersonal element of good: both Griffith and Svengali were *teachers* and taught their charges to earn a living. It is important to bear in mind the economic element in the careers of those Hollywood somnambules whom I shall discuss later.

The *nervous* somnambule of Lillian Gish is hardworking, although her type, considered with reference to society and to the characters she portrayed, is less competent than a very recent successor: Vivian Leigh. *Gone with the Wind* and *The Birth of a Nation* overlap in many respects. Both had heroines victimized by the change the Civil War brought in its wake; both were brutally awakened from the feudal dream into a post-feudal reality. Both endured great physical rigors. But Scarlett O'Hara, prophetically, was much more a modern woman, a more complete psychological and social type. Miss Gish was incidental to the theme of her story, whereas the theme was incidental to the personal story of Scarlett. What is Scarlett but a feudal Eve who passed through the Lilith stage into a *stage* ruled over by Tallulah Bankhead as the termagant heroine of *The Little Foxes?* Scarlett learned to con-

trol her nerves; therefore she seems nothing but a
Lillian who was initiated into a sophisticated personality by events. If Miss Gish had not been so active,
she would roughly correspond to Scarlett's counter-
foil, Melanie. Miss Gish, however, was hardly more
than a stylized dream, a somnambule with the jitters.
Women who are ashamed of desire (and this is the
generic, psychologic base of the Gish formula) cannot
forever feign a pseudo-somnambulistic isolation—unless as actresses they should become figments of the
romantic genre itself: dream characters, metaphysical
symbols, heroines of Poe. As an artist in pantomime,
Miss Gish could be as enchanting as anyone I have
ever watched; her art was unimpeachable, her charm
intense. Her modern counterparts, strangely enough,
are foreigners: Elizabeth Bergner and Luise Rainer.
Yet in comparison with Miss Gish, these actresses are
sophisticated and more human. The course of movie
history dealt Miss Gish a harsh but poetical fate: her
heroine of *Broken Blossoms* (the Gish-Griffith chef-
d'oeuvre) was but the somnambule debunked—beaten
rather than hypnotized into her "ideal" state of sexual
readiness.

Phoenix-like, the somnambule's myth arose from
the frail, lifeless body in the Chinaman's arms to dominate in several curious forms the sexual industry of
Hollywood. Actresses from abroad have brought new
styles subtly inflecting the Gish tremor and the Bara

undulation of sex-consciousness. The importation of foreign stars was absolutely necessary to the expansion of the love-romance film, the growth of which was coincident with the general growth of Hollywood and the "art" of the movies. The great female stars of Hollywood, as soon as the foreigners began to arrive, were characteristically "women of passion"; that is to say, they became the heroines, whereas before they were "villainesses." Norma Talmadge was one of the few female stars of fairly mature and average characteristics who could compete with such players as Mary Pickford, Marguerite Clark, and their mythical galaxy of chastity and charm. The first important foreign actress, the one who changed the tide, was Pola Negri, who could not, however, reproduce her continental successes in America. This was owing largely to the ambiguous way in which Hollywood understood her talents: she was cast in semi-vampire rôles. The truth was that her histrionic realism was alien to the artificial pattern of the Hollywood tradition of the vampire. The point is that she was *not* a somnambule, she was not a neo-Gothic symbol. Hollywood ended her career by casting her in an Irene Bordoni rôle.

As long as her spell remains potent, the Hollywood somnambule thinks perpetually in terms of her own myth, the myth Hollywood has fashioned for her, and is indifferent to all others. *Indifference* is a characteristic of the sleepwalker as it is of sleep. When sleeping, we immunize ourselves to the outside world, and when sleepwalking, we parade that immunity. The paradoxical quality of the elision of the somnambule with the woman-of-passion is that a certain immunization from sex is combined with passionate desire: a desire which must have at least the superficial appearance of activity. Garbo appeared on the Hollywood horizon as a rich emissary of this peculiar ambivalence between chastity and passion. She corresponded, as a matter of fact, to the American taste for symbolism in sex, for a dramatic arrangement of chastity and passion conforming with the vestiges of the puritan tradition. Hollywood's wizards correctly sensed the Northern asceticism in Garbo and divined its true mission. The extra-curricular images of Garbo's loosely tailored suits and mannish shoes by no means disappear as essences in her cinema portrayals. Her grace is angular, no matter what she wears, and her personality emanates a subtle frigidity. On the screen in terms of character, this spiritual quality has the appearance of "restraint," namely, passion held in restraint—a "deep and smoldering" passion. Such a conception of Garbo's passion, however, is far too pat, superficial, and, indeed, "literary." Not even the boys in the back of the balcony believe it.

When a woman of passion is portrayed in the movies (a unique instance and a moving portrayal were given by Elizabeth Bergner in *Dreaming Lips*), American audiences misunderstand it in proportion to the lack of "sizzling hot" embraces and innuendoes of the bedroom. Hence Garbo's métier of the woman-of-passion inevitably and gradually became the kind of burlesque which I designate as the charade. The pantomime of Hollywood somnambules tends to be statically conventionalized (like the movements of national dance forms), and when they lend themselves to the creation of such a specific form as a character, they tend to transform the movie they are playing in into a charade. Garbo, play-acting passion to the hilt, created nevertheless a somnambulistic kind of detachment. The audience as a whole senses this unerringly without being aware of its structure, and the usual reviewer can do no better than call it "mystery" or "remoteness," or—at the most radical—"frigidity." After all, there are mysteries of sex life which Hollywood does not treat, from the most metaphysical, such as that treated by Balzac in Seraphita, to the most technical, such as those dealt with in the psychoanalytical clinic.

The sheer power of the somnambule's personality arises from the social situation which it connotes: frigidity in a woman of beauty or charm is a direct challenge to male sexual vanity. Garbo's peculiar art has been always to say in essence to the male audience: "Don't forget that I am only an image, and that that is all I can be to you; in fact, it is all I would be even if you, instead of Ramon Navarro or Melvyn Douglas, held me in your arms." *Even if* . . . that is perfectly true. Still, such a conscious thesis in an actress's work would not account for her devastating effect—only the accidental presence of the somnambule's image accounts for it! Men sense the rigidity in Garbo's spine, are aware of the broad, squarish shoulders deliberately hunched and the long, poetically prehensile arms of a growing youth; therefore, when she bends her head back, revealing a neck as lissom as a white goose's, there is an *ambivalent* reaction: her orthodox defenses are down, her will against seduction seems to melt, at last all her conscious, instinctive reluctance disappears . . . A few moments of pantomime rehearse the basic natural drama of sexually uneducated woman and sexually educating man.

But Time is inexorable. Somehow, the most flamboyant successes become, like weapons of warfare, anachronisms. And Garbo's face, Garbo's somber, elusive charm, joined the anachronisms. The box-office barometer, tardily enough, began to fall. Hence Garbo had to start all over again with the American public. She was always wise about publicity—at least, her wisdom was temporarily practical. She needed mystification no less than mystery. Her large feet and mannish clothes, however, received too much publicity and had a corrosive effect: as the mystery became stereotyped, the mystification became too evident. In that plodding way the public has, movie audiences began to wonder about the meaning of Garbo's "private" assets. They read she was girlish and unaffected off the set. They read that in real life she had lighthearted romances. The moment had come when the mystification had to be elucidated, since the mystery had already been liquidated. Hence *Ninotchka*, in which Garbo's private style of dress became transiently her public, or professional, style. The movie's plot followed the pattern of her "private" Hollywood legend of preoccupation and standoffishness. In it she was cold, absorbed in her work, distant from pleasure-loving society, and oddly enough, she came as an emissary from that home of a new society, Russia. Ah, she was a revised somnambule of a revised steppes! She obeyed a Svengali called Stalin until a realistic American came into her life and awakened "the woman" in her. Now at last the narcissistic appetite of the American public is satisfied: Garbo, paragon of individual exoticism, has been initiated into the national lessons of *Vogue* and *Harper's Bazaar*! She has entered the shopgirl's paradise: *imported* chic. A strange Americanization for a foreign actress: a fall from the true "Paris" model to the original, American Paris-emulated model. How timely Hollywood was—connecting its greatest star with the destiny of hats on the eve of a war which isolated Paris from the fashion world!

The sado-masochism of the public was obviously aroused when Garbo gave a belly laugh from the region of that remarkably monosyllabic pelvis, with its boyish imitation of the Venus de Milo. This was made clear by *Ninotchka* and its successor, *Two-Faced Woman*, in which the star not only laughed, giggled, and flirted like Ginger Rogers, but danced a version of the rumba and appeared full-length in a bathing suit. The audience mercilessly kibitzed Garbo's kibitz of Garbo in the comic plot of a sportswoman's attempt to keep her new husband's love by imitating (via a mythic twin sister) the city sirens he is used to in his urban business life. Such are popular triumphs—for the audience. Garbo is unbelievably inappropriate in all but her sports getups, and even one of those is bold, bold Bonwit-Teller. For his designs, Adrian seems to have peregrinated between the Fifth Avenue and the Broadway chic shops, turning out a negligee that would sell for five dollars at Klein's on Union Square. The star swishes around in them, like Bette Davis before she learned how to walk from chair to table in front of a camera, and dances with astonishing lightness and grace for one who seems to have lead in her heels. Constance Bennett, who plays in *Two-Faced Woman*, can give her hammer and sickle and still win out as more human. Garbo's other face is no less artificial than her first one; in fact, it's much more so.

But the issue is an apparent Hollywood attempt to Americanize its culture at a psychological moment in history, and the method is in concrete sense "anti-artificial." Garbo at last appears with eyelids bare of false lashes. She is being made re-available to the many by a kind of stripping. Even her voice is becoming egregious by dislocation from the traditional Garbo personality. During *Two-Faced Woman*, I closed my eyes in order to experiment, and Garbo's voice sounded like a chipper little grandmother's. If Hollywood goddesses, somnambules, and so on cannot be transformed, they necessarily must yield to younger rivals. Dietrich, too, had to go through a sort of metamorphosis in order to revive her box-office divinity. But in her case, since she is more morally commonplace than Garbo, it was a matter of keeping the pattern but gently lowering it to another level of dignity. This was accomplished in *Destry Rides Again*, the comedy-romance version of *The Blue Angel*.

Dietrich, more than Garbo or Crawford, has emphasized the recognizable moral values in Hollywood somnambulism. Crawford is a pure product of beauty parlor and dramatic school, and thus there was a perfect symbolism in casting her in the rôle of a woman whose life was ruined by a scar on her cheek. The scar itself is symbolic of "natural" ugliness and plainness, which the nation's beauty parlors are sworn to destroy. This movie charade was symbolic in still another way: Crawford's public is being addressed much as was Garbo's, if more tentatively: "Do you want our Joan as she is—or shall we start to rehaul her?" In the sense that any girl who wants to reach the top in Hollywood must eliminate all personal prejudices and desires, and submit herself passively to the Hollywood factory of beauty and style, every actress in the movie city is a sort of Trilby . . . a Trilby who may or may not be talented enough to act the rôles she pleases after two or three years. Dietrich, just as much typed as Garbo, "clicked" by a more obvious route. She is what the boys on the street corner sartorially describe as "class." To put it more comprehensively and tactfully, she is the Carnal Woman in distinction to the Woman of Passion. Both European, Dietrich is more typically so than Garbo, who brings a draught from snow-capped mountains. The superiority of the European brand of siren goes beyond her greater sophistication as a woman and human being. She has a literary, social, and theatrical tradition, and this invests her inevitably with a humility in the center of which is a superb assurance of her rôle as an instrument of love. Dietrich has this exceptional humility, which too frequently passes for chic swagger or mere pose. That Dietrich preserves this quality through the thick and thin of her artistic fortunes attests to its universality. To compare her rôle in *The Blue Angel*, however, with that in *The Scarlet Empress* or another of her heavy glamor parts is to observe the process of her *somnambulization*.

The bedroom morality of a Dietrich heroine is always precisely the same: vague. The only rational conclusion about many of her rôles is that she would certainly be a lady of easy virtue (even if she isn't) if she could ever bring herself to be really promiscuous. Though sometimes the story gives one the right to believe she *has been* promiscuous, her life is changed or threatens to be changed by the entrance of a unique male who arouses in her a sentiment of pure love (observe that this is a reversal of the Garbo legend). Dietrich's public has relished this almost mathematically set theme ever since she began to make American pictures. Its popular attraction is unquestionably the delicious ambiguity of fact that she enjoys all the sensations of promiscuity without necessarily having to go to bed with anyone! Thus the somnambulistic ritual: she is a carnal woman who sacrifices her proved nature to chaste behavior temporarily or as an experiment; that is, she creates a charade of virtue while apparently she has undergone no basic change of personality. It is as though, for the benefit of her man or her public, or both in one, Dietrich consents to an initiation rite into pure love, a rite which (she sometimes carefully warns her prospective mate) may or may not transform her. What is the implication for a male spectator who has no special desire to hypnotize a woman in order to get her to sleep with him? It is that Dietrich would have been ripe *for him* before

John Wayne or Gary Cooper came into her life to limit her activities by offering marriage. The American ethnic conscience requires obeisance to its two gods: Money and a Decent Home; namely, a proper standard of living honestly paid for. Dietrich is a siren who consents to behave chastely while she is directly in front of the altar of the American conscience. Her somnambule—charming, subtle, of an infinite twilight wisdom of Lilith—is obviously prostituted to an idea rather than to the opposite sex. The idea is that, if she were not just hopelessly "bad," she would enjoy the privilege of marrying a nice American and having a couple of kids . . .

Given its premises, Hollywood is most wise! As long as personality is a problem in the clinical sense, and assuredly it is just that today, the problem of good and evil is hopelessly compromised and may be manipulated with bold symbolic freedom. A dated, and non-Hollywood, manifestation of this moral ambiguity was R. L. Stevenson's Jekyll and Hyde fable. In its own terms, Hollywood has a "literature" parallel to the sophisticated creative treatment of personality problems in Gide and Pirandello. If it were not for Bette Davis, however, it is doubtful if Hollywood could be said to have furnished a concrete case of modern neurotic somnambulism. Miss Davis has many times portrayed sexual neurasthenics in plots

more or less revealing the technical portent of character, and thus she appears as the inheritor of the Gish
tradition, as a veritable jitterburg of tragediennes. She
has never sought to soft-pedal her pantomimic pro-
clivities, and these have tended toward the crystalliza-
tion of a nervous, sharply high-lighted style, mixing
petulance, acerbity, infantile emotionalism, and whimsicality. This style has nothing necessarily to do with
her stories, being as integrated with her spontaneous
physical movements as were Miss Gish's quaveriness,
flirtiness, shyness, and naïveté. Miss Davis seems only
a Gish grown older and wiser, aware that her early
illusions of sexual innocence (somnambulism-of-the-
chaste as a social value) are wretchedly inadequate
but still unable to do altogether without them. The
Davis personality, while advertising itself as the common "maladjusted" type, is brazen, strong, and consciously willing to meet society with what weapons it
has at command. This was distinctly brought out in
Dark Victory—in which the moral problem, however,
was resolved in a physiological debacle. A satanic
flavor (an anti-somnambulism) exists in Miss Davis'
typical heroine: she is like a woman who has been
awakened from an unconscious state to discover that
she has been ravished, but who suspects that the
"somnambulism" had a measure of her own complic-
ity, and thus has a perpetually unsolved psychological
problem. The paradox of casting Miss Davis in ordi-

nary rôles requiring a purely dramatic working out of a psychological problem, of course, is irrelevant to Hollywood specifications. Though Miss Davis' neurotic style has a certain legitimate reflection in the literary material given her, I cannot eliminate an image of her as a perverse somnambule who perpetually purges herself in a dramatic crisis false to her true character. It is the awe-inspiring secret of Hollywood that its dramatic situations, while superficially plausible, seldom solve the problems they are supposed to solve. Like much second- and third-rate literature, this is to present the pre-drama, and is related, as I shall show at length in a later chapter, to a static conception of drama in art and morality in life. In the movies of Hollywood this is not so significant as it is in modern novels, since the cinema terms are basically hypocritical, a romantic camouflage of the real problems.

While Garbo and Miss Davis are slyly unavailable in sexual rôles, Dietrich and Mae West are slyly available. Of all the ladies with sleep in their eyes, Miss West is the most complex—but if she is the most complex, Hedy Lamarr is the simplest. Miss Lamarr doesn't have to say "Yes," all she has to do is to yawn. A surrealist imager, Joseph Cornell, has isolated the purely poetic quality of this somnambule by casting her apparently empty beauty and unquestionable impression of nocturnal acquiescence in the personality of the opposite sex. The somnambule Hedy accepts even this imposition with astonishing placidity! Mr. Cornell cut her face from one of her photographs and imposed it over the face of a young painter of the *quattrocento* in a reproduction of his self-portrait. Her beautiful eyes do not protest from amidst the alien hair of the past, and the tingling torso does not rise up from the seat of the opposite sex. In her perfect will-lessness Miss Lamarr is, indeed, identified *metaphysically* with her mesmeric midnight captor, the loving male.

Once she portrayed a showgirl (not a chorus girl) in the movie *Ziegfeld Girl*. This animated odalisque of American theatrical history, the showgirl, is the purest somnambulistic type of all. She neither speaks nor is spoken to; she appears and disappears more inadvertently than the dream; she is loaded with diamonds of the imagination and rubies of hoarded blood. The most fantastically unreal costumes not long ago were invented for her, merely to distract the attention from the fact that she was actually clothed. Her gait is strictly standardized; it is a gliding, rhythmic somnambulism . . . The strip-tease girl of burlesque is but a step and a shake toward "waking up" the showgirl; namely, toward achieving that reality of sex which the poorer man finds necessary for his evening hallucinations, since he cannot buy—even in the imagination—the shimmer and sheen of the showgirl. The strip teaser is only the somnambule tipped off that she can't get away, like the showgirl, with being passive and statuesque; she must actively evince the symptoms of sexual readiness and even seem to undress for the sexual act. A further step toward such "reality" away from somnambulism, and yet still in the ritual-symbolic mold, is the device of the female impersonator. Because nature has not fitted him for the *waking* rôle he really desires, and because he cannot imagine that rôle satisfyingly in his own dreams, the female impersonator imitates the somnambule. His experience takes him, however, from the showgirl stage to the strip-tease stage and beyond it in an agony of frustration, because, although he is often, if talented and attractive, relatively successful (though he has almost disappeared from the professional theatre), he cannot realize in private life those sterling functions which would give him a necessary impartiality toward his artistic charade. Thus, every time he puts on his female masquerade, he must realize the whole gamut of somnambulism I have just outlined *in one evening*—from the astral vision of a Hedy Lamarr at the top of the stairs to the strip-tease girl doing "the bumps" at the bottom . . . and finally, perhaps, be reduced to that blushless order of advertisement from which even women usually cringe. It would be difficult to imagine a sexual type that would rescue the *purgative somnambulism* of the female impersonator from its context of devastating reality and render it paradisiacal and esthetic, but such a type actually arrived in Hollywood from Broadway: Mae West.

As with all somnambules, Miss West's infirmity is instantly recognizable to everyone, though not always correctly identified as such—namely, as a symbolic or dream form. It is remarkable that one may think of her as a joke, or a freak even, but not, except through sheer snobbery, as an objectionable woman. The most amazing thing about Miss West is her good humor. She herself has said, with more perspicacity than a thousand cinema scribes, that her popularity rests, or at least rested, on the fact that everyone believes in her *goodness*. Assuredly, it is a goodness more convincing than that of any of her competitors, for it has large quantities of the maternal in it. Her particular charade is fairy tale, and astoundingly impertinent. In her films, she was the Bad Girl who was always a Perfect Angel. Her instinct for ambivalence was as neat as the magnificently simple style she created to express it. Her goodness was the goodness of everyone's mother in the most elementary and orthodox sense, whereas her badness, so mysterious to the uninitiated as to induce many to call her "sexless," was a purely mimic badness. Miss West dared to add a legitimate dash of humor to the myth of the Œdipus complex.

No doubt she observed the female impersonator and, spontaneously imitating him, extracted for herself all his comedy, leaving him his pathos. In effect, she expunged the *burlesque* quality from his active masquerade of the female sex. On the other hand, she implicitly placed on the altar of his seriousness the one supreme sacrifice of female nature: the mother's recognition and condonement of the homosexual flaw in her son! This, of course, almost never happens in life; that is why it had to happen at least once in art. Only one convincing symbol to embody this condonement is imaginable—for her to *imitate* the ritual of her son's excess and perversion: a ritual which, she recognizes, may be but the ironical counterpart of her own perverse repression of sexuality, or else a straightforward reflection of the same depraved desires and their realization. Thus came about in Hollywood art the most extraordinary and insinuating somnambule of them all.

If you will analyze the simple but subtle hieroglyph of Miss West's physical style, it is possible to identify the gestural traits of all the somnambulistic types I have mentioned. Her gait is considered inimitable—only a unique synthesis could be so inimitable. At first glance it seems to be a disrespectful emulation of the Lillian Russell era of feminine charm, a Bowery version of a Florodora girl. But its idiom is too creative for that, its intonations are too distinctive. Miss West's poise, identical on every occasion, no matter what, is inevitably carried out, while it corresponds to nothing in life. It *suggests*, however, mellowed and reassured, the hysterically stylized movements of the female impersonator. Moreover, though few may have noticed it, Miss West is as lazy as a snake. Yet she is always a showgirl, and, just as paradoxically, she is also always "on the make." She is too dignified to do "the bumps," an activity which she reserves either for her eyes or her voice. Again, it would be audacious and unconventional to call her delicate, yet her delicacy has the status of a duchess's concern for the formal respect due her; in this sense, she is an illustration from Ronald Firbank. Like Lillian Gish, albeit anachronistically, she assumes in her person and without self-consciousness the prerogatives which a fragile female once believed, if she had been reared properly, were accepted by a sympathetic and gentle world. She knows what is, or was, due a lady, and wouldn't take guff from Garbo. She is also, inevitably, mysterious; when she smiles and rolls her eyes up, I think of Mona Lisa and the Sphinx; that is, of the banalized classics of mystery.

The strip-tease girl is forced to exaggerate the showgirl, and the female impersonator is forced to exaggerate the strip-tease girl—this is the minimum rôle for the somnambule; after this, there must be different dreams, different gestures, a different style . . . That I find the somnambules the most attractive symbols of femininity is a purely personal prejudice. But I must assert that I have not tried to determine here

Hollywood's prize winners in general sex appeal or realistically negotiable charm. I have tried to explain the mechanism of the charade—to analyze a phenomenon peculiar to the movie city. Only Hollywood, with its complete tastelessness, could have leapt the chasm between the somnambulistic female impersonator—so intent on "waking up" to a new reality—and a visible and animated symbol (in Mae West) which could bestow on him a secure *somnambulism* and, through an art of maternal understanding, rescue him from that vulgarity into which the somnambulism of the unmarried woman (imitated by him) had consigned him in America. The scandalous sway of Miss West's hips—it reminds me of nothing so much as the motion of a cradle; it is hypnotic, soothing: a finished and flawless equilibrium . . .

CHAPTER V

THE GOOD VILLAIN AND THE
BAD HERO

BETWEEN these ambivalent poles—villainy and virtue —the most striking types of Hollywood hero have been stretched, their voluntary suffering being the better borne as they are mindful, during the intense spiritual and physical suffering they undergo, of the reward that lies at the end of the torture: their salaries. The zest for living and high adventure which is displayed by so many protagonists in gangster melodramas and historical romances—this feeling I have never been able entirely to dissociate from the type of self-confidence a man exhibits to the world when he is certain of a well-paying job in the movies as well as certain of his ability to survive the final blank from the gun that (if he enacts a gangster) is presumed to kill him. I do not depreciate the talents of Edward G. Robinson, James Cagney, Humphrey Bogart, and others of the sympathetic bad man type (a type, even as I write, some-

what senescent), for they have brought a certain vitality and character to lines on the screen that might
easily have been void of interest and ingeniously performed rôles obviously cut from the identical piece of
whole cloth, fitted with but few alterations to suit
their personal idiosyncrasies. Nor do I point with inadequate sophistication to the fact that the Hollywood gangster hero has often been a bad man sugared
with the sanctity of vulgar sentimentality. For to this
charge might be opposed: "But you, who have complained that Hollywood does not treat seriously
enough the problem of good and evil, now deplore
that both the traditional beloved rogue and contemporary 'good man gone wrong' are absurdly ambiguous
—apparently just because the actors are well paid for
their work!"

I bow my head. It is true. I realize that the greatest
heroes of all time have been sinners in the conventional sense, and that the protagonist of Greek tragedy,
the most significant ethical type in Western art, may
be viewed as gathering unto himself the moral burden
of mankind: he must (even as Jesus Christ) martyr
himself for the sins of others and be stretched between
the very poles I have mentioned, villainy and virtue,
before the critical yet sympathetic gaze of an audience,
realizing that, as the hero is a symbol for society, so
is the individual actor but a symbolic vessel for the
characteristics of the hero. It is not that in its own way

Hollywood does not recognize the existence of the problem of good and evil, it is that its terms are artistically disingenuous, and that, though realism either of a romantic or naturalistic sort may be intended, the result is nevertheless apt to be charade-like, of an allegorical crudity.

At first sight, it would seem that the moral struggle of the criminal, especially the dude gangster, is foolproof and, barring obvious fictional devices, realistic enough; namely, has a rough proportion of truth, a fair adherence to the facts. Certainly Hollywood is not to be chided for having spared the rod and spoiled the gangster. But this was a journalistic realism, and the obvious fictional device was to present the criminal as a weakling or a "pure victim" of circumstance. Such was the moral thesis of two of the most famous of Hollywood's gangster melodramas, *Public Enemy* with James Cagney and *Scarface* with Paul Muni. A third, *Little Caesar*, unequivocally indicated vanity as the vice supreme and posited the guilt of the Napoleonic complex (current examples, Mussolini and Hitler), which in its most serious aspect, hinted even by Hollywood, is the inferiority complex. Thus, evil, as obediently typified by Hollywood tradition, is the result of deviation from society, its laws and conventions —among which, incidentally, is a decent standard of living. In fact, with respect to this last, Hollywood does not depart an inch from the sacred platitudes of criminology; the criminal element arises from social maladjustment owing to lack of education and to temptation practically fostered by poverty. The "heroes" of the rod and the stiletto-glance emerge as such notorious examples because of extreme personal daring combined with extreme personal vanity. They are outstanding victims of an "individualistic illusion"—a romantic belief that they can "beat the game." Thus, psychologically, they differ in no degree from the beloved rogue type of pre-cinema fiction, from the Homerian Ulysses to *The Prisoner of Zenda*. The swashbuckling heroes of Douglas Fairbanks, Senior, were early Hollywood examples of the fascinating scoundrel who won the ladies' hearts and yet was by no means morally irreproachable; especially two of his heroes are classically significant: Robin Hood and Don Juan. What may be called the Robin Hood motif is the most comprehensive, perhaps, that could be assumed to motivate the beloved rogue, and of course Hollywood has not failed to exploit the theme of benevolent villainy also in regard to its gunman and racketeer heroes. There was always love or loyalty to a henchman, a sister, a mother, or a virtuous sweetheart to do duty for salving the criminal's conscience toward society. In *Scarface*, it is a sister who brings out the only humane trait in the character of the gangster, who in every other respect reveals himself as a cheap show-off and a profound coward.

It certainly seems not only artistically conventional but natural to humanize such a type-villain as the gangster, with his journalistically stereotyped traits. But it should be recalled that the gangster is, to begin with, a somewhat limited symbol of social nonconformity. He does not represent either a heresy to some subtle ethical custom of society, such as the extra-legal relations of the sexes, or a conscious rebellion against economic, political, or religious laws. That is, the gangster is an "unethical" sinner, he does not deviate through principle but through some muffled necessity; moreover, he is not, like Raskolnikoff, a borderline case, a man who commits a crime for esthetic-ethical reasons, partly out of an inner necessity to experience a certain emotion, and partly because he obscurely perceives an incongruity inherent in the processes of legal justice. Raskolnikoff's metaphysical principle, that of experiment in sin, touches strangely upon both the decadence of Greek drama in Euripides, whose "humanism" questioned the authority of the gods, and the pseudo-ethic of the modern gangster, who kills for a thrill. Both Scarface and Raskolnikoff are modern and sceptical to the extent that they are individualistic, and in this sense emblematic of the romantic hero developed in nineteenth-century literature. Even as Rhett Butler of *Gone with the Wind*, they have a "cavalier" attitude toward what respectable society considers is fixed, absolute, and thus sacred, whether

it be God or the Republican Party. I visualize Raskolnikoff as a man somewhat Einsteinian in his sensibility, one who apprehended somehow the hidden complexity of the criminal's guilt; that is, observing that
the criminal deeds of murder and theft were sins
against both God and society, he perceived—or *in-
tuited*—a discreteness, a confusion between these
points of view toward crime—namely, God's and the
police's. Raskolnikoff somehow imagined that God's
retribution should be as persistently and emphatically
material as that of the police's: a purely logical and
practical, rather than ethical, issue. One cannot ac-
cuse him of lack of spirituality, yet it would seem that
he missed in sensible observation, not only a *logical*
retribution, but even the basis for the Christian assumption of God's protection over the innocent and
His precaution against the impulses of the evil. Truly,
the police are not omnipotent, they cannot prevent
crime, but they can punish it. Thus the ironic title
of Dostoievsky's novel, *Crime and Punishment*,
whereas its real theme was, paradoxically because of
the inverted order of the words, *Crime and Pre-
vention*. Raskolnikoff's tragedy was that he could
carry through the crime as logically as the police could
pursue and capture him, the criminal. The only true
cancelling of the crime was that of the police, which
is why he accepted it fatalistically, even saved the
police the trouble of pursuit. Dostoievsky's grim moral

was: If not the pre-cancelling of God (the sensibility of Good), then the post-cancelling of the police (the sensibility of Redemption from Evil).

The economic rôle of the romantic hero is that he is out for what he can get; whether it is inside or outside the pattern of legal conformity is of no account to him, but the extremity of his emotions nevertheless logically carries him beyond the boundaries. His inspiration, as in the case of Don Juan, is often sexual, and thus a greater ambiguity of immorality attaches to this sub-type than to those who, such as the gangster, endanger a kind of material property competed for on less humane terms: money and private property other than women. Although a large portion of society frowns or pretends to frown on wife-stealing and husband-stealing, fornication and adultery have tacitly been deemed essential to the working of the social order, particularly since the post-Victorian "emancipation" of woman. A certain purely humane, free form of sexual competition exists, and condemnation of transgressors against sexual morality takes the form of social exclusivism of various degrees of harshness, but is not in the large sense to be termed "legal." Briefly, one cannot go to jail for stealing a woman's affections unless, to effect the theft, it has been necessary to murder her husband, her father, her brother, or her sweetheart. Without requiring a metaphysical sensibility, the movie gangsters have always recognized that it was The Law they were up against, and the meta-physical aspect of the law which corrals a cinema Dillinger on a mountain top is no less and no more inexorable and "absolute" than that which corraled Raskolnikoff in the office of the police inspector. Both are physical processes presumably set in perpetual mo-tion until they attain their end, the apprehension of the criminal, and meanwhile they have the united ethical approbation of society as well as the assistance of "every decent citizen."

A dynamic law of living has it that all forms of ex-cessive passion or moral extremism are self-cancelling. But an intuitive awareness of this law has never de-terred those who are seriously tempted to be extreme from fulfilling their natures. After all, it is experience which is desired foremost by human beings, and if moral problems exist in society, making it natural for art to depict them, it is not awareness of "inevitable retribution" that should deter the heroes of drama and fiction from action, for then art would be homiletics; virtually, it would commit suicide. How curious it is to note that suicide is the precise metaphysic which governs the moral flavor of gangster sagas as well as of Dostoievsky's great novel of crime—for does not Raskolnikoff's behavior constitute a sort of suicide? Ah, but it is a *moral* suicide, a true expiation, an ex-change of a sense of Hell for a sense of Purgatory, and therefore not self-extinction except in the dramatic sense of a change of identity. Yet what is the expiation of the gangsters who have died in a hundred Hollywood movies? Indeed, the hollowness of the art of movie gangsterism is that the moral experience is lacking—the sense of the nature of crime is lacking. Thus the sociological dictum that ignorance produces crime is socially true but dramatically and esthetically defective. Œdipus was a genius; it is only that he lacked a single point of information: the identity of his mother and father.

Why—and here is Hollywood's journalistic realism —do, not only screen criminals, but actual criminals sometimes have to be dragged "the last mile"—why do they whine, beg for impossible pardons, or sit in brutal apathy? Because they cannot understand why they are being punished, that is, because they have the amoral inflection of the beloved rogue, the same romantic adventurer whose individualistic social nonconformity is an ethic of "I (namely, the ego) am good and society is bad," without realizing that a dialectic must exist, that every individual is a result of social forces. It could be argued that "society" is substituted by the gangster and the beloved rogue for "the father," but one should not begin by making the mistake of assuming the family-complex is isolated from society! Jean Jacques Rousseau's "dodge" that the secret solution lies in a sort of spiritual nudism merely placed the pagan tradition ineffectually behind the ego . . . The sentimental gangster (always with a dash of Robin Hood if not Rousseau in his moral complexion) is a confused person who believes that right is might insofar as the individual and only the individual goes; if he has a few friends who like to be ordered around, all the better. This is largely the result of narcissism, but how can we morally evaluate narcissism? The question is too broad for Hollywood.

An important recent event in the cinema city is the transference of the romantic emphasis from the criminal—though he still clings as the "gentleman thief" or a shady detective (*vide, I Wake up Screaming*) — to a revival of Tarzan and the introduction of Superman: one of their chief traits is an obviously justifiable narcissism. The social defect of Tarzan is that he is still too rural; it has taken him too long to adapt his prowess to the conditions of urban civilization, a sequence Hollywood has seen fit to imitate by its casual production of this series. The fact is, Tarzan is too much inflected toward certain more romantic, almost ideal, aspects of life isolated from reality; his jungle paradise, for instance, is a reincarnation of the Eden myth. On the contrary, Superman derives his supernatural qualities, which ally him to the airplane and the cannon themselves, directly from the city in which he appears to have been born and always stayed. He has a reporter's job, and the only credible explanation of his muscles is that he developed them in a gymnasium, though this hypothesis could not explain his superhuman strength and preternatural psychic and neural capacities. His importance in the popular imagination is testified, not only by Hollywood's hiring him, but by the many dozens of imitations of him in comic-strip literature. In one way, he is the logical inverse of the gangster hero; he is out to counter gangsters and their gangs; he is also the sublimation of all detective heroes, while at the same time he is not associated with such an unsavory place as a police court. His solution of evil is not merely superhuman, it is super-social. In not accepting the realistic conditions of society's struggle against crime, he symbolically does not accept the moral premises of normal human efforts to correct and prevent crime. It is now a commonplace of comic-strip, cinema, and radio melodramas that individuals who take the apprehension of criminals into their own hands (even though, like Superman, they may fly through the air with the greatest of ease) are disliked or somehow distrusted by the appointed guardians of the law. This is no romantic convention of melodrama, but a logical reaction realistically founded. The moral significance of Superman is that he is a disrupter of normal official order through the possession of exceptional faculties and perceptions, and it is inevitable for different moral ideas to flow from such an equipment when it is placed by the individual owner at the service of his own whim. What *is* a romantic convention, however, is the self-less aspect of Superman, his apparent lack of personal problems or even private satisfactions. Especially dangerous is the "superman" attitude of individuals in the case of international war, for then the adventurer, the beloved rogue, interested, as I have pointed out, only in his personal prowess, is a potential "man without a country" and, hence, may be enlisted by any class, nation, or individual who happens to attract him or offer the highest pay. A man of this ilk is potentially the most morally dangerous a society could possess, depending upon his degree of talent. Thus it is only in the popular moral sense that Superman is the gangster turned inside out. More truthfully, he is an extension of the narcissistic gangster to the point where his individualistic lust to exceed the strength, daring, and self-glorification of other men is visibly and neatly satisfied by attainments which brook no comparison and which nature herself mysteriously (and unassisted by society) supplies. Society, in the eyes of Superman, does not have to be overcome in order for him to be glorified. Having been born glorified, so to speak, he has only to overcome those men having false and delusive individualistic excesses—the criminals. Notice that substantially this is Hitler's message to the German people: a "super-race." But, as I have just said, in the case of war between nations, in which the good-bad distinctions are turned topsy-turvy (prisoners were released by the Confederacy to fight in its depleted armies and promised freedom), it is the superman who becomes the potential criminal! —even as Lindbergh, that superman of the airplane, became the object of black suspicion when it appeared he might be a sympathizer and collaborator with Germany. It is no romantic conceit that many versions of Superman appear on the newsstands today with red, white, and blue stamped on their tights, and it surprised no one when Superman began to fight on our side.

Hollywood cinema has actually supplied the real gangster with that mythical glory which was an indispensable part of his dream, and which connects him with Raskolnikoff in the consciousness of those who understand, not only to what degree Raskolnikoff has nothing to do with Scarface and Little Caesar, but also to what extent each is involved in the social creation of the criminal. Is it not largely a question of taste? Yes, taste is all that can rescue us from a purely literal distinction between Raskolnikoff and the others —between Raskolnikoff and, for instance, Spade, the private detective of *The Maltese Falcon*. Certainly an inept association of ideas is bad taste. But it is not bad taste to analyze the internal mechanism of inept associations of ideas. It was not inept for Raskolnikoff to

kneel in the streets, confess to God, and then hurry to
the police station. This is a purely ethical type of glorification. But it is inept for Hollywood to invent a parallel process for the gangster, who may or may not
confess, who seldom confesses to God, and who never
hurries to the police station. The gangster, like the
beloved rogue, is only melodramatic. His death may
have pathos, but it is the pathos of human misery
which any newsreel is equipped to give us if it so
choose. The artifice of such a death lies in the cleverness or eloquence of the sympathetic personality in
Hollywood who may be impersonating an ignorant
scoundrel. The movie city believes that to *humanize*
is to *glorify*—when that suits its convenience; its
method may also be to ruralize, de-humanize, and
super-humanize.

It is well not to be too dogmatic about these gen-
eralizations. Human courage, the determined endur-
ance of suffering, has a certain moral virtue and a
certain power of appeal; one spontaneously pities the
sorely harried and the close beset. But these are minor
considerations which Hollywood treats as major. It is
the old tear-jerking tradition. A startling and relevant
proof of all this is the absurd American production
accorded *Crime and Punishment*. After the Russian
and French productions, it was sheer vulgarity. And
why was Hollywood at such a loss to make anything
out of Dostoievsky's "original script"? Simply because

there was no place in it for that violence which urban movie audiences find necessary to make them feel "at home." Let us admit that gangster and detective melodramas, adventure stories of all types, satisfy a perpetual latent craving in the American psyche for physical expression, for a type of energy that humdrum factory and office jobs have no way of releasing. After all, the gangster's choice, though neither conventional nor "reasonable," is somehow profoundly wise. It gives him a personal weapon of noise and action; on him and with him, the machine becomes personal—an extension of his physical nature—and he orders people around with it. The illicitness of his incontrovertible power corresponds to the illicitness of the employee who would like to tell his boss to go to hell, and if he doesn't like it . . . The gangster is also "amusing"—he is a *little* Caesar, and the audience knows this very well, not only because he seems marked by fate for destruction from the beginning, but because they intuit he is overrating his personal powers, is a "cocky" personality, an extreme narcissist; they love it the way they love a spunky child or a small boy who very irrationally takes on a couple of big bullies. It is adorable, but adorable because, like some of our own petty illusions, it is a romanticizable illusion of the weak. As for the gangster's ignorance, that is so forgivable to the nonethical movie audience! If ignorance were the crime, then it would be the crime of the audience, who represent society. From the view of an enlightened ethics, ignorance is that bliss which exists until compelled reluctantly to pay a price for knowledge. Hollywood should have been persuaded that Raskolnikoff was not *bewildered*; Peter Lorre, who played the part in the American version, submitted to the Hollywood interpretation of Raskolnikoff as naïve, frightened, and puzzled . . . and no wonder, with Marian Marsh playing Sonia.

Hollywood crime has been well or knowingly done only when it has had recourse to violence, in which it is expert, not only for temperamental reasons, but because effects of rapid and cataclysmic action are especially adaptable to the cinema medium. *San Francisco*, for instance, despite its absurd characters and story, was impressive purely because of the camera's reconstruction of the physical debacle. Here was the thrill of becoming intimate with physical events without actually participating in them. This business of eavesdropping on earthquakes—is it not quite analogous to becoming intimate with a gangster's fate? It makes little difference, so far as the audience goes, *who* is on the receiving end of the bullet or *who* will sit in the electric chair.

The prime device for cinematically creating a gangster hero has been to counterpose his outward violence, addicting him to gunfire, to his inner gentleness, addicting him to love. It is true that he was tough even in his tenderness, which is natural enough, but it is clear that his toughness was but the clumsiness of a certain social class. At bottom, he was as sentimental as the next guy, who may happen to have the advantage of being born into a better family and have had a better education.

Hitherto, I have talked of Hollywood's good villains almost exclusively; I shall now notice its bad heroes— that is to say, the ones who have had enough education to detect which is the side of the angels and which the side of the devil, and whose choice of the former has been somewhat ambiguous. From Œdipus to Superman, it is not hard to see that the man in whom good qualities are developed (that is, educated) to truly heroic proportions is socially undesirable—in an extra-criminal but still ethical sense. Œdipus' wisdom was as much a challenge to the gods as Superman's strength to credulity. Whereas Superman's is a fantastic myth (like that of Philoctetes, whose strength in drawing the bow aroused the jealousy of Hercules), Scarface and Œdipus have realistic myths. Thus, Œdipus was not a criminal who was made much of, but a man who was much and made a criminal— being created indirectly through his excess of good qualities. Thus, he was a "bad hero," an educated and virtuous man who somehow had to suffer for the sins of an unevenly developed and *inwardly disharmonious* society. As an old man in exile, he complained that it still puzzled him why the gods had made him suffer for something which he did ignorantly—the legitimate complaint of a man who had no *human* technique for foreseeing the disaster that would befall him: killing his father and marrying his mother. And to the end, though still god-loving, Œdipus was bitter and defiant.

The differences between the good villain and the bad hero are esthetically manifold, and yet they form the human circle; in the hemisphere of the former we find the gangster hero and the beloved rogue: Hollywood individualists who, although they retain lovable qualities as individuals, are voluntary exiles from "good" society and re-enter it only out of motives of irony or gain, to mock or plunder it. Thus, as they operate socially, they are ignorant of that type of collaboration which is considered essential to society's welfare. In the other hemisphere, what has Hollywood to offer? Very little, for in this sphere lies the tragic destiny of the hero, who falls from the height of social grace to the depths of social disgrace or to death itself. A villain (Iago is an ideal example) is one who realizes his inferiority as an absolute limit to advancement into the highest state of social grace, and yet whose pride will not allow him to accept his weakness, his hardship, lying down; he will scheme to overthrow those who exist in the envied state of grace. The romantic hero of the satanic variety (Byron's heroes, for instance, and Des Esseintes) are individuals who stand an even chance of attaining the highest social grace but who, while they refuse to be saints, renounce "good" society in order to lead a more exciting, glamorous, dangerous, or secret life. The romantic, so to speak, takes the fatal leap before he is toppled . . . He is still a good villain—one might say a *damned* good villain. Hollywood's "pure" villains have always been Iagoan, and powerful, as a rule, solely through money. The nearest thing to an orthodox bad hero in Hollywood is Gary Cooper, whose purity is tainted by his rural ignorance, his lack of worldliness—but this taint is always richly overcome by the actor's personal charm, a fact which makes Cooper and one or two others wholly artificial with relation to actual society. The fact is that men of "charm" with the rube's viewpoint on civilization are usually professionalized—like Will Rogers, or, to skip to another field, Edgar Guest! Of course, there persists a weird fallacy, on which Hollywood bases much of its output, that to be naïve and gullible and sentimental is the essence of the human—and is "heroic" because inescapable. Alas, alas!

As for pure heroes, besides the obvious pair of young lovers, with the male's human, all too human, faults, Hollywood of late years has offered us the Benefactor of Mankind, the scientific inventor and discoverer, thus veering skillfully to the side of genius, knowledge, and education. This type has been surefire, since, far from being romantic in the individualistic sense, men such as Pasteur, Zola, Bell, and Ehrlich (all of whom have had screen biographies) were visionaries of social good and carried on their work specifically to identify themselves with the common destiny. The moral would seem to be that the Devil disappears before the advancing footsteps of Knowledge. But how many human beings can be thus heroically "self-sacrificing"? First of all, it requires genius in a specific, objective medium: an art or a science. What did his education, his general culture, avail Œdipus so long as he could not please the gods as well as he could rule the people of Thebes? Society favors only the producer, and then only so long as he manifestly produces, fits into a broad, practical scheme: that is, so long as his public character is identified with the prosperity of the community. The road of individualism is beset with grave dangers to the hero who reaches for the highest social grace.

Considering Œdipus as one whose "business" it was, like that of modern presidents, dictators, and kings, to govern well, the essence of the hero may be defined as a super sort of professionalism. All men desiring greatness in the public eye (including actors) undergo a difficult discipline and the acquisition of an elaborate system of knowledge, whether medicine, law, government, or a fine art. But for the sake of considering the subject matter of art (morality) rather than its form (esthetics), we must turn to the direct rôle of morality in society—that is, to the doctors, the political rulers, the inventors, and so on—rather than to the writers or actors who depict them. Œdipus, a great king, erred fatally in his private life. A blemish on a great man's character may be forgiven in enlightened times but, in the strict ethical sense, it declasses him as a hero—unless he be a good villain or a satanic hero, the devil triumphant. All societies covertly accept the underdog, the unredeemed wrongdoer, the little fellow, as a hero—but on the esthetic rather than the moral side. Sin is sometimes "pleasant." Superman is a professional in the physical skills of man—his physical and mental athleticism. A great actor is an adept at acting a large variety of serious rôles. Some Hollywood actors attempt to be such heroes (Charles Laughton, Paul Muni, and so on), but without any notable degree of success. It is much more natural to cast them, therefore, as good villains, romantic fellows who, so to speak, reject the commonplace morality of a "mere job" to enter the "profession" of piracy, gangsterism or, most dubious of all, beachcombing. Thus the step of Hollywood heroes from virtue to villainy is parallel, strange as it may seem, with the step from a *job*, which is commonplace and routinized, to a *profession*, where competence has a certain creative aspect, or at the least, definite elements of individual initiative, judgment, and imagination. The body of an actor's art is no less broad and general, while still under individual control, than is the great doctor's or lawyer's. But suppose that in acting stereotyped gangsters or adventurers, the actor's art suffers, itself becomes "villainous"? Acting then tends to become a "job" rather than a "profession" and is declassed in the way that a safe cracker's *job* is a demeanment of a racketeer's *profession!* At the same time, a racketeer is villainous just because, ethically speaking, he evades the conventional virtue of holding a job.

Such speculations are in direct line with three fairly recent screen heroes: Chaplin's Dictator, Orson Welles' Kane, and Spade, the private detective of *The Maltese Falcon.* All these men, from the Hollywood viewpoint, are good villains caught red-handed in the first reel attempting to be bad heroes. Having submitted, apparently, to one esthetic-moral doctrine as screen types, they have arbitrarily adopted for their respective, particular films a new aspect of personality. The first fact to strike us in considering the three (I exclude for the moment Chaplin's Little Barber) is that each is a stock villain somehow found in the hero's place, the temporary place of social grace. Yet by this token they do not become good villains, for they are plainly not, as are the gangster and the beloved rogue, melodramatic and stereotyped. They are individualized characters—and Spade, indeed, reverses the villain-into-hero motion. For although as an actor his personality is molded on gangster lines, he enacts a private detective, someone on the side of the law; in this case, the ambiguity is less obviously the result of the type of man characterized. The dictator and the master-financier are, after all, types around whom a nucleus of public disfavor has grown, whereas the private detective is a sort of psychological surprise, a strictly up-to-date revelation. But let us examine these amalgams separately.

Hitler started out by being a villain; that is, as a common man he was on the losing side and felt weak, inferior, and dishonored. Then he became a political conspirator: another kind of villain—and what, in a sense, are all three men, Hitler, Kane, and Spade, but conspirators plotting to force upon society a consideration of their personal qualities, their peculiar kind of education, their "belongingness"? Hitler was a "romantic hero" of a kind in his Austrian days; he was exiled from his homeland, and was violent, seething, restless: he longed to return to Germany and become a "pure" hero. This honorable redemption of the fallen hero is a familiar enough theme, but one which in itself Hollywood has never taken at all seriously; by chance (though not altogether by chance), a few Hollywood artists have been original enough to vaguely perceive its importance. In Chaplin's case, oddly enough, it is for more or less hidden autobiographical reasons. First, he himself is a Jew, and must in his early life have associated his difficulties with being a member of that race. But finally he came to the top of the social heap through art: that is, with the peculiar weapon of his knowledge. But this, Chaplin plainly sees, is his individualistic triumph which, coupled with the fact that outside of Germany it is common to think of Hitler as an individualistic case, a megalomaniac, gave Chaplin a perfectly *coherent* impulse to play Hitler. It should be interpolated here that the actor's contribution to the common good is not only transient but unique in its ratio of individualization to socialization. But Chaplin obviously could not put into Hitler all that he (Chaplin) is *as a man*, while it is equally evident that he could neither put in him all that he is *as an artist* . . . Thus came about the conception of the dual rôle. As a general thing, the dual rôle fascinates actors because it is seldom indeed that an actor expresses his entire personality by his art of human portrayals. On the other hand, *The Great Dictator* would have been much more interesting artistically if the Great Dictator and the Little Barber had had a scene together, but aside from the risk of an artificial effect in the double shots, Chaplin neglected the opportunity because he did not concretely realize that in acting the two rôles, he was splitting his personality. This is the moral motivation of his assumption, in the final scene, of his personality *as a man* when he puts aside his motley (both as Dictator and Little Barber) and becomes a small, middle-aged, embarrassed but courageous Jew, making a liberal plea in behalf of his race and all humankind. The effect is tremendous—but not just as Chaplin intended it. Suddenly, one wants to look anywhere but at the screen. Here was the Man abdicating from the Mask of the Clown purely for the sake of making propaganda. Was there not a grave irrelevancy here? Was this irrelevancy not a misunderstanding of the real relation between art and society? Chaplin's art is comic. The clown he placed on the heights is a mousy sort of man, an underdog, a universal type whose antics are perpetually moving because they are the acme of incompetence and unworldliness. Gary Cooper's incompetence is too realistic, that is, too capable of being educated and turned into social currency, cheap profit. Mr. Cooper has been starred in the Deeds, Smith, and John Doe pictures, wherein the Common Man has been turned into the Great Hero overnight. But poor Charlie has always sought a mere job! Hitler also had this difficulty, but it happened that he created for himself a very big job—to conquer the world, on the basis of having become a super-professional politician. Likewise, Charles Spencer Chaplin became a super-professional actor. The moral significances of their respective professions, both attained by extreme mastery of technique, are wide apart, not only in *The Great Dic-*

tator but in society. As adepts, both Chaplin and Hitler are "pure" heroes; they benefit vast numbers of people—or, as to the latter, such is the illusion of the German people at this time as well as hidden groups elsewhere. In the purely esthetic sense, both men are great creators of movement. But in stepping from the rôle of the Little Barber directly into the rôle of the Dictator, Chaplin bridged the impossible; one man's art could not do both clowns any more than one man's morality could do both professionals. So, in the end, one had to step down—and the one to do so, of course, was Chaplin, the professional actor, who in the gesture became Chaplin, the man. As a comedian, Chaplin has always been the good villain, the shiftless, romantic little bum, who nevertheless wished somehow to be united with society. Since in *The Great Dictator* this little person has a barber's trade until an organized social force puts him out of business, his step from the good villain to the bad hero—from the tolerated romantic bum to the "intolerable" little barber—becomes visible. Morally (and Mr. Chaplin is intelligent in this respect), he had to place himself in the position of Hitler's typical victim, the common worker; hence, he had to be both a "professional" worker (an artist) and a mere job-holder. Hitler, in the movie and in life, had evaded an ordinary job, his course having taken him through the sub-professional romantic adventure to the orthodox "great profession" of ruler of a nation. But Chaplin wished a moral judgment against a professional hero with the wrong ethical and political philosophy. He became the fool in the king's place with satire as his scepter. On the other hand, since in real life Chaplin is a ruler of his art, he does not escape leveling a finger at an aspect of himself as the artist who has formed a professional dictatorship over the little bum, who, even as the small business-man, has become *typed*. As rich and unique a conception as this clown is, perhaps he is *isolatedly* unique and somewhat *overrich* with perfection.* Is he not strictly complementary to the dictator of real life, Citizen Kane, and thus indissociable from him?

The theme of a lonely dictatorship is also manifest in *Citizen Kane*. An entirely different conception of this movie I shall discuss in a later chapter, but here it is the central figure which is relevant. While he is obviously patterned to life, this fact in itself is of no special interest. Kane is a man who has made a huge success of the financial business of living and yet who had a great private passion and a great frustration—I use the term "great" ill-advisedly, for the simple reason that I use it strictly in the Hollywood sense of super-production; and, indeed, it is on super-production that the Kanes of real life base their "heroic" statures. Welles' point was to show the emptiness of soul which dwelt in this love-mad collector of *objets d'art*. Welles'

* Mr. Chaplin has recently said, "The tramp is dead."

expert camera is trained upon the transitional stage of *good villain into bad hero* more realistically than Chaplin's less self-conscious camera. Here is a single individual who, as an entrepreneur of yellow journalism and a piler-up of profit, has earned a romantic treatment from Welles' hands, the same "humanizing" biographical treatment given gangster heroes. Thus the gift of good villainy is first bestowed on Hollywood's "Kane." But finding himself a good villain, Kane, as it were, and I can see how his spirit was tempted by young Mr. Welles' cherubic countenance, felt inspired to trespass on the territory of the bad hero. He desired a tragedy, an "ending" in the grand style. He dies in his modern castle, alone, eaten by despair, clutching to him the only memory he has saved from the vast and hollow pretensions of his life: a bauble which reminds him of his boyhood sled and his innocent happiness as a child. The scheme is gaunt enough to be tragic, but unhappily it is also naïve and basically phony. Owing to the insuperable obstacle that every moment of his adult life Kane is manifestly a vulgarian and merely goes through the mimetics of tragic frustration, Mr. Welles' movie is reduced to the artistic importance of a flower pattern on a shaving mug. It is chic to have one on the mantelpiece. A hero must fall from a great height, but Kane's obsessive passion for the girl he makes into an opera singer, no less than his spiritual resurgence to the past

in the form of childhood fetishism, is strictly a hy-
draulically elevated, studio height. What a true charade!—and with Kane forced to impersonate Orson
Welles . . . It would have been more interesting if
Mr. Welles, dividing his personality as neatly as did
Mr. Chaplin, had portrayed Kane the dictator and
also "himself" as the struggling young actor who
dares to impersonate him. Then, at least, we would
have had comedy, rather than something which is
neither fitly foul nor good red hero. A good villain
may vulgarly cover himself with as much blood or as
many ornaments as he desires, but, unless he be also
austere, he cannot be a bad hero.

Spade, the private detective of The Maltese Falcon,
through his austerity comes poetically close to being
a bad hero. His austerity seems the result of his steer-
ing a delicate course between being on the side of the
law and opposed to it. So remarkable are the plot and
characters of this movie and so excellently are four
leading rôles played that an independent and vital
personality emanates from it—an actually creative
flavor, a most rare thing in Hollywood. Spade, bril-
liantly brought into being by Humphrey Bogart, is
limned in the very image of a gangster hero, but with
an unusually fine and acrid edge. Spade's power seems
to derive from a kind of moral decision as the result
of a complex emotional struggle, a struggle that evokes
the Dostoievskian heroes of crime and compassion—

even Muishkin himself, as well as Dostoievsky's most "contemporary" hero, the Man from Underground. The last named is the man who understands that his doom is to look at life from beneath and envy what is above, to squirm and do nothing about it but complain; he is the neurotic finally deprived of a sense of social solidarity: the prototypic paranoiac. The interesting thing about this conception is its static verticalism, the awareness of a narrowly extensive but heaven-aspiring hierarchy like the one Kafka's hero, K., perpetually seeks to join. K. is the automatic exile, the "hero" who has never been permitted to act, to exist in dynamic relation to the orthodox hierarchies of society. But there can be neither hero nor villain in the true sense unless there be action, unless man either finds for himself a usual place in society or creates an unusual one, at home or abroad. The citizen's relation to the law, explored so exhaustively by both Kafka and Dostoievsky, must, to be dynamic, involve a dramatic attitude toward law, *a basis of action*. Save in his last novel, *Amerika*, which strangely resembles the plot of a Chaplin movie, Kafka avoids this element, and as a result his stories are neo-allegories. Dostoievsky created a character corresponding to K. in the Underground Man, but at least he took a sardonically comic view, made him a clown, whereas K. is even deprived of the privilege of suffering like a clown.

Spade's occupation as a private detective places him in a highly strategic, dialectical position toward society and its orthodox values. Openly, as a professional, he is against the lawbreaker, and, in order to keep his job going, has to play ball with the police. But is not this thereby merely an *economic* bond with the law? Is Spade not really bribed each time he accepts a client's fee, not only in the sense that he works privately and may for the sake of a client (as he does in this movie) withhold information from the police, but because his license permits him to enter the confidence of clients whose reputations and dealings would otherwise be at the mercy of official, public justice? Thus, cast in the orthodox temperamental mold of the gangster hero, the good villain Spade avoids being sentimentalized because of an ambivalent orthodoxy—an ambivalence that permits him to have sympathy or contempt for his clients, and also friendliness or hatred for the police. Thus he is an ideal example of the visible metamorphosis of good villain into bad hero, and capable as well of juggling these categories while he is in action; for he may be a good villain to the lady crook at the very moment he is a bad hero to the police department, and vice versa! When he is being a good villain to the police, when he finally traps the crooks and dutifully hands them over, he is being a bad hero to the woman and her

gang of co-plotters—he is betraying his previous rôle
of her benefactor.

Alas, he does not love her, and his ability to detach
himself even from love, as well as from all the other
emotional appeals his clients may make to him as a
human being, is based on his moral temperament as
an underground man, one who, out of some mysterious
necessity, cannot socialize his emotions, cannot throw
himself into the drama of admiring and being ad-
mired, into the mystery of believing in values and
participating in their crises. Yet some vestige of human
emotion, eager and curious, having its own strange
brand of sentimentality, draws him toward the underdog, the fellow in a scrape, the fellow whose happiness
or reputation is threatened, the fellow who is afraid
of the official law. *This* is why he is a private detective, for he divines in the hapless underdog the victim
and suspecter of what he himself suspects and of
which he is a victim—the law. He is the law's victim
because he cannot, even as Raskolnikoff, detach himself from it, flout it; and, like Muishkin, he feels some
inexhaustible well of weakness in himself which forever binds him to the suffering and the helpless, to
the naïve believer in, or victim of, a moral value. I felt
Spade's large and sentient pity for the woman as he
mercilessly baits her in her apartment while trying to
extort her secret. She interests him because he wants

her to be sincere and he thinks she isn't; he is unconsciously confusing a sexual motive with a professional motive. And later, in the highly touching love scene, when he declares it is only good business to avenge his partner's death (he now knows she is the killer!), he adds that, anyway, he could never trust her if he let her off and married her, since he has something on her, and, who knows?—she might put a bullet in his back some day. Here his relationship to Muishkin becomes very clear, if only by the devious way of a unity of opposites. Yet Muishkin, too, had an unconquerable shyness which operated practically as moral hesitation, a magical sort of detachment from normal social life, which he vanquished only through an almost "messianic" delusion of grandeur. Spade's messianic impulse (the woman is a sort of Mary Magdalene) is perverted into mental sadism; his catastrophic symptom is not epilepsy but masochism—emotional self-denial. Why does man not believe in values, why does the flag of values not carry him headlong into the midst of human experience, to live or die under that flag? This is a profound human mystery. Today its manifestations are largely concerned with *the legal*, the basic constitution of human society.

Ignore the law? Be yourself? Oh, yes. Assuredly. But that takes a certain toughness, another backbone, a certain uncompromisingness of desire which neither Spade nor Muishkin has. That Spade should be a softie of this kind aligns him with our other subject, Kane. Spade exits from the picture carrying the phony statue, the supposed value of which all the trouble has been about. It is within the essential plot, not only of the movie but of his character, that the Maltese Falcon should be a phony, for all along it has symbolized those values of life Spade scornfully and shyly associates with the above, and which ironically the law is designed to protect, just as it must protect the tremendous collection of art works accumulated by a vulgar Kane. But Spade, poor soul, is a naïve romantic in comparison with Kane, who is bluntly sophisticated. It is only Spade's idiosyncratic delusion that the *genuine* work of art is symbolic of values, for consciously he does not realize this. As remarkable an archaic piece as is the genuine Falcon statue, it has value for Spade, as for the crooks, only because its lead coating is supposed to conceal a fortune in jewels. The jewels are not there. And because the crooks too seem interested only in the money, Spade despises them. Spade won't break the law; the jewels wouldn't be *his*. But the crooks, as Spade does not perceive, are interested likewise in *adventure*, in a certain glamorous mode of living, in the value of breaking the law. They are romantic good villains. Unlike Spade, Kane respects all the premises of the law, even to the bottom of his soul, and takes every technical advantage of them to enrich himself. What matter if his appreciation of art has only the motif of conspicuous consumption? What if, in this sense, he is very like Hollywood itself? His gang, the other capitalists, have played ball with him, even though, as a "lone wolf," he has often fought groups of them; in this sense, he has been conspicuously companioned, and warmed. It was sexual love, personal love, that did not warm him, or at least not properly. Yet he batted in the same league. It is Mr. Welles' rather foolishly sentimental myth that there is no warmth, no spiritual substance, amidst the economic gregariousness of the Kane breed. Any close and numerous assemblage of financial digits generates its own warmth. Kane obviously got a lot of ordinary pleasure from living. He believed for a long time in his gaudy fetishes; they, too, had an undeniable warmth; they incarnated his spirit. Of course, he was neither sensitive nor very intelligent; he could not be expected to tell one work of art from another in any informed sense, but if so, neither could he tell one sled from another—unless it belonged to him. It is true that he made the mistake of hiding the true warmth, the sled, in a sort of arctic attic of the mind. But then, Mr. Welles is wrong: the sled is not a true fetish. On a different level, the psychology assumed in Kane is that of the seekers after the statue of the Maltese Falcon. The fetishism, the value, is supposed to lie irrelevantly *under the skin of the object*; the form is largely a lie.

If this is true, Kane is not a tragic, but a melodramatic, hero. At least, it is evident that the romantic crooks always had the *object in view* and thus are more interesting and more intense than Kane.

Spade, intelligent enough to stand in some awe of values, and creating a recipe to deal with them in practical life, is tactful enough to work alone. Kane did not work "alone" out of tact, but desperation, and basically did not depend on himself but on the monetary system. In the fatal sense, Spade had to be a private detective, for it is perhaps the one profession where one can work alone and feel truly self-reliant, where one can exercise individual initiative, imagination, and so on, without assuming the hero's plan for individual self-glorification in the eyes of law-abiding society. Spade is a quibbling Satan, a Robin Hood who doesn't steal anything but the glory of the police—in a way, he even adds to that glory by giving the credit to the police department as a whole rather than to the police chief himself! Spade stands in a sort of hinterland between the job and the profession. He is criminal, psychologist, detective in one. But he also has the sense of "doing jobs" in the manner of the petty crook or the plumber. Perhaps his true job is to keep himself human . . .

Indeed, here is formulated the "job" of Hollywood professional actors, who humanize themselves by taking the rôles of job-holders or those who evade jobs by adopting illegal or adventurous professions. However, the actor may slip over into the realm of the "illegal," the "villainous," to the extent that he does not rise above the level of hackwork in his profession. Many Hollywood actors are racketeers of pantomime and voice—more or less clever, more or less inept. Sometimes a virtuous acting equipment is put to villainously small use (like that of John Garfield), or sometimes acting one type so much, even if doing it well, makes the profession déclassée, makes it seem like a job. Under such circumstances, actors' salaries are likely to seem excessive, and hence the good-evil content of their rôles to seem secondary to their heroic money-earning capacity. Thus, the size of a salary may be in comic disproportion to our understanding (via Hollywood) what is villainous and what is virtuous in society.

CHAPTER VI

OF MICKEY AND MONSTERS

Mickey Mouse is the antithesis of Frankenstein. A perfectly acceptable analogy would be David and Goliath; indeed, I am pretty sure that Mickey once played the redoubtable giant-killer. The antithesis is basic: Mickey is tiny and agile, Frankenstein is huge and unwieldy. They belong to the same allegorical class by token of their marginal relation to the animal kingdom: Mickey is of the Æsop genre, whereas Frankenstein, being, inversely, the debasement of a man rather than the aggrandizement of a beast, is the plausible hero of Mrs. Shelley's anti-materialist fable of the soul and body. As dichotomies, they have the same traditional drama of irreducible antagonism: body-soul, animal-man. The genius of Æsop was to show by a comic allegory, clothing a serious human situation, the effectuality of spirit. With a grain of human intelligence, given their simplicity of instinct, the animals could reproduce the experience of mankind in illustrations a schoolboy understands. Æsop, of course, was a dialectician of the transmigration-of-souls doctrine, the purpose of which was to prove that man is a higher form of life, and that in dying he does not cease, he only proceeds to a lower (more elementary) form by continuing his life in the body of an animal.

Mickey, as Hollywood's leading representative of the Æsop tradition, is soundly comic, his animation being a logical development of the comic-strip sense of action. The great humor of Mickey and his confreres, Donald Duck and so on, is based on rapidity combined with economy, a principle which also governs human beings in factories, for it is in the latter that speed, directness, and skill count most when the human organism is not engaged in the sports arena or on the battlefield. The antics of the animated-cartoon beasts are by no means always laughter-provoking. Our satisfaction is comic in a deeper sense—something in the way that Molière affects us, it is the pleasure taken in observing a miraculous simplification: a wise puppet-show of the emotions. But it is not altogether, in Mickey's case, his parody of human nature which pleases so completely; or rather, his parody partakes of a very special and contemporary form of human nature: man's perfectly serious parody of the machine in factories and offices. Observe that the Disney studio is literally a factory. Of course, it is an esthetic platitude that the basic pattern of comedy is parody of the machine, but even this relatively recent conception does not seem really adequate in this case. *To be mechanical* is, after all, not precisely the same as *to be mechanized*. First of all, Mickey Mouse and the others are, like clowns with collapsible costumes and soldiers with guns, "mechanized": fitted out with a machine, their machine being the cinematic principle of "animation." Just as we saw the ease with which the Hare, in Mr. Disney's brilliant rendition of the well-known fable, performed as a mechanized "idea" of speed, we see Mickey perform as a mechanized "idea" of David; with the machine, they do things which otherwise would be impossible. It was David's expert use of his primitive weapon that won the battle against Goliath, and the inspiration to use it arose from the desire of the human spirit to overcome material odds in brute nature. If the Hare lost the race, it was because he was a show-off: he preferred the form to the content, and thus the profound defect of Æsop's moral is that it offers no means of evaluating the result of *winning;* namely, what is the permanent value of the *prize?* Mickey, however, uses his machine-donated agility to outrun, foil, and vanquish the most fearsome monsters.

At the same time, an ambiguity lies in the fact that Mickey also *is* a machine, namely he is a mouselike image which is subject to perfectly mechanical laws manipulated on paper at the will of his creator, Walt Disney. He is also a vessel with an allegorical content, but for all his pre-existence in painting and literature, he did not before have at his disposal such a perfect "slingshot" as cinematic movement. In having this weapon, this element of agility which is so much superior to man's, he assumes, together with his legend as a being persecuted by man, a certain ominousness, a queer illusion of independence of his creator; he is so fabulous an acrobat!

I recall one of the first animated cartoon efforts in American cinema; he was a clown, and he used to emerge from and go back into an ink bottle, leaping from this womb as mature as when he returned to it. I also remember that, mixed with his antics, was a most insouciant defiance of his creator to catch him and put him back in the bottle; no matter what took place in each successive film, the identical interplay followed: he had to be captured and reincarcerated all over again. Sometimes his creator would torment him by leaving a part of him undrawn; that is, sometimes he would begin on the paper, and there were glimpses of the artist chuckling with amusement at the impotent anger of the little man, perhaps demanding his other leg so that he could begin his performance.

This drama between creator and created is the basic pattern of the Frankenstein myth—the monster created in man's image who, lacking a soul, is aware of it and, resentful, turns upon his maker in wrath. But why is one serious and the other comic? Because in the pen-and-ink clown, the old principle of the parody of the machine prevails. Whereas Mickey illustrates the comedy of the mechanical resources of the underdog, Frankenstein is the late nineteenth-century myth of reaction against mechanization—mechanization, that is to say, as an enemy of the human spirit rather than its ally. Today, in the world drama of war, we see exactly this latter situation: mechanization as an agent of destruction, and the German and Japanese armies in the esthetic guise of so many million "Frankensteins" while our own boys are "Davids."

But let us look at what Hollywood did with the Frankenstein legend. By having to use actors and making the story a melodrama, as indeed it was largely conceived by Mrs. Shelley, the movies transposed the body-soul pattern, its ostensible moral import, into the man-animal pattern—the more "esthetic" meaning and an inversion of Æsop. Boris Karloff, as Frankenstein's monster, is a standard, subhuman convention of the cinema city as well as Mrs. Shelley's character; that is, he is one of the folk symbols of rape. A picture which takes this crude melodramatic slant leaves quite open the question of the relation of the machine to man, whether it is valid to consider that it has the same *subhuman status* as the animal to man, or whether man's dependence upon it is permitting it to usurp the human.

The Shelleyan inversion of Æsop (brute instinct in man's body) is but a latter-day conversion of the trans-migration-of-souls myth. When man's spirit dies, it lives again in the mechanized body, and then this curious machine begins to *live*; that is, it becomes "animal." This—one criticism of mechanical civilization—is an inversion of the comic principle of man imitating machine: it is machine imitating man. According to the esthetic of Mickey Mouse and company, this is still comic to the extent that at the bottom of the Disney hierarchy is inanimate nature; the first Silly Symphony, *Trees and Flowers*, was an arboreal parody of the human, and even dead nature is revivified by the animated-cartoon genius—cutlery, books, playing cards, and so on.

But, as I have said, we react to the animated cartoon on a certain serious, *unhilarious*, level as well as on any other. What is this deep pleasure of ours in Mickey's hair's-breadth escapes, managed partly through the most astonishing skill, and partly through a curious kind of coincidence? For it is as though the world of nature, with its purely physical laws, should—apparently out of a humorous sense of benevolence—conspire to threaten Mickey with annihilation only to save him the next instant, and over and over again

. . . I think of him on the bicycle, and the nonchalant cat on the other end of the plank onto which he rides, as the plank seesaws over the abyss of the river: a cartoon in which the innocent cat (intent on food) seems to symbolize this mock-tragic whimsicality of benevolent nature. Morally, it is tonic to think that the mechanical being of nature, the mathematical operation of all its physical laws, can respond so winningly, so *musically*, to the physical ardor and grace of man himself! But, beyond this "musical" reciprocity, we must consider that the "man" is really a mouse, and so has a special symbolic meaning. *Are you a man or a mouse?* goes the proverb, which means, Are you strong enough to fight material odds in the open or must you resort to the tricks and subterfuges of the weak? Must you, in other words, develop skill as a defensive technique?

It is of the profoundest irony that in the case of war, in which whole nations of men organize against each other in a life-or-death struggle, the machine principle prevails and synthesizes the maximums of skill and power. Alas, then! Mickey is a *peace-time* morality, his only analogy in the world of war being a small and plucky nation such as Greece—and we know what happened to Greece. But in the more pertinent sense of his myth, Mickey is the peace-time individual, indulging in a dream of pure escapes from material dangers in which at the same time he has the most strenuous fun. Consequently he represents sport as a morality, no less than morality as a sport . . . When the mechanical principle is symbolically dedicated to the consummation of peaceful happiness and delight in leisure, its protean joy becomes wonderfully manifest. Then its coördination of deliberate skill with spontaneous reaction is on an esthetic-moral level; it is musical and profound. The spectacle produces in us soundless laughter that is the laughter of irony in a world of grim seriousness. For we understand perfectly in the depths of our being, as we watch Mickey or that acme of futile and amusing rage, Donald Duck, that it is man in nature who may cunningly divert its mechanical principles toward objectives of destruction.

The title of this chapter parodies a title of John Steinbeck's. The movie made from his novel, *Of Mice and Men*, was in some ways a very slick affair. Indeed, the original literary conception suffered, not so much from clumsiness, as from that grossly disguised vulgarity which passes in the popular theater for "drama"; by mixing melodrama with "character-study," a bastard sort of drama may be achieved. There is some shrewd observation and invention in Mr. Steinbeck's opus, and this is quite evident in the movie, but, like so much popular fiction (and I include the more serious variety), it is the interpretation of the material in terms of concepts that invalidates the realism—or, since *Of Mice and Men* has so many realistic devices that, largely for cinematic reasons, succeed, perhaps I should say *spoils the reality*. The finally disastrous element of the movie is its effect of a "realistic" Frankenstein-monster in Lennie, the huge cretin. His normal pal, George, is at pains to reveal to society that he alone is responsible for saving Lennie from the authorities, and thus is as morally responsible for the girl's murder as Frankenstein's creator for the deeds of his monster. Why hedge? Lennie is George's *thing*. There is no other force that motivates the cretin other than a pitiful kind of animal intelligence; in Lennie, in fact, we get full-fledged just the ambiguity I mentioned above: a crossbreeding of the two antithetical schemes: man-animal and machine-human. In the movie, the ostensible truth is that George is a boon to Lennie, that he checks, soothes, and consoles him, as well as manages him; in short, that he is the civilizing force in the brute's nature. But how subjective, naïve, and radically false is this evaluation of George's —for it is his and the author's, not the spectator's or reader's. On the contrary, George is molding the free form of the brute: the brute released, as Frankenstein was released, into the world of men and things. To have given Frankenstein a zealous and tyrannical nursemaid (which is all George is to Lennie) could not have saved him from perdition any more than (Mr. Steinbeck is the authority) it was able to save

Lennie. Like Frankenstein, Lennie is overcome with emotion in the presence of what is living, soft, and defenseless. As Frankenstein could pause to dandle a flower above the fluffy head of a little girl, Lennie loved to cuddle rabbits and mice.

The conception of a bona-fide, flesh-and-blood Frankenstein, whose tenderness is logically isolated from his brutality, is revoltingly vulgar. The original blame must go, I fear, to the scientific fallacy of contemporary fiction: the attempt to introduce sociopathological categories into character creation: a fallacy to which Mr. Steinbeck fell victim. Even so, he is astonishingly superficial, because, from the pathological view, George is much more profoundly ailing, and much more "dangerous to society," than Lennie, who achieves a rapid and absolute extinction. The integuments of George's problem are firmly knit with so-called normal society. The Lennie-George relation as imagined by Steinbeck-Hollywood is definitely pre-Freud; it is obvious that George's emotional pattern is to seek other Lennies. He is not only a sentimental bum of the American road, but a sentimental bum of the American mind, and unconsciously perverse. His dream is a little farm, not where he can raise a family of human beings, but where Lennie can have all the rabbits he wants to pet. Did not Mrs. Shelley's doctor also have a "dream"? Did he not believe that Frankenstein was the inhabitant of a future heaven-on-earth?

When the impossibility of realizing such a dream was forced on George by events, he, like Frankenstein the creator, understood his duty. It was *kill the monster.*

The inference is simple. If the cretin Lennie, who theoretically is the recipient of our sympathy throughout, be viewed as a mechanism controlled by George, he becomes repellent and monstrous. But so, at the same time, do the mice and rabbits he fondles, so does the girl whose humanity avails her nothing in Lennie's arms, for they are but the grist for a machine. Ah, Lennie loves! And there's the rub, for this love is only the disguise of rape, and hence but another weapon (and how ambivalent a weapon) in the arsenal of the subconscious. For a purely *logical* sadomasochism, of which rape is the *emotional* symbol, is inevitably destructive. As nature benevolently seems to conspire with her mechanical properties to create an *illusion of danger* for Mickey, she malevolently seems to conspire to create an *illusion of safety* for the mousy creatures who come tame to the hands of a Lennie.

Can we, however, leave Lennie as such an unsympathetic and troublingly tragic brute? If we exclude the murderousness, the potential explosion that will come, we can almost sympathize with the couple, George and Lennie, in their extreme pathos as havenots, unfortunates of the road, inheritors of "the grapes of wrath." Let us try to open our spiritual pores to the most human and conventional aspects of the forlorn two, Lennie and George, let us gradually transform them into shapes more akin to their own "orthodox" desires for happiness. Let us first forget they are of the same sex, and remember that Lennie is perfectly female in his dependence on George, that his economic rôle cannot exist without George's masculine organization. He can work like any plow horse, but he must be tended like one. If he could have cooked, he would have been perfect. But George could cook.

In choosing Lennie as a future domestic companion, George is not very far from the sensible and commonplace motives of the average American male. One has often heard men of humble economic status complain of being unable to find a woman suitable for the home. Having a woman around means the sexual problem, it means a type of moral obligation which a surprising number of males are ill-equipped to afford these days—a moral and financial obligation. A pretty woman is the thing to have in a home, but the prettier they are, alas, the less useful they feel they ought to be.* Charlie Chaplin has a perfect solution for this in *Modern Times*: the dream. Charlie's wisdom, like George's, makes no bones of the wish situation, but fleshes it forthrightly. Sitting on the curb in front of

* Of course, the present war has sensibly modified "the domestic situation."

a vacant lot, Charlie experiences the ultimate heaven of imagined happiness: a little cottage with Paulette Goddard in the kitchen, grapes (not of wrath) growing in the window, and a cow who comes to the back doorstep to be milked.

Oh, yes, Charlie has a job, a humble one since he carries a dinner pail, but not too humble. Just humble enough. For the cottage is a spiritual cocoon in which is woven the silk of dreams for two—Adam and Eve. Of course, the silk is really cotton, but that's only American industry, and right now, only patriotic. Charlie is more of an artist than George, however; he knows when to draw the line, and prefers a pretty woman and a dream to a real cottage and a human work horse. What a pathetically grotesque elision of desires we have in George! His psychological malady is compensation; his social malady is hyper-economizing; and his sexual malady is symbolic substitution. Lennie has more points of contact with Paulette Goddard than appear on the surface. He is docile and faithful—at least, Charlie's dream makes Paulette docile and faithful. Contemplating such a curious parallel, the mind goes back to those days of the cave man, when a male had to knock a female in the head and drag her home before she could be domesticated. At least, so we have been taught to believe. And we are reminded (without laughter) that Lennie was knocked on the head when he was young, an accident which made him as available to George as the primordial female was to her mate.

A part of the magic of the movies is the unconscious irony, the twist of reality, the arabesque of fancy which makes thrice real an inferior, vulgar fable such as Mr. Steinbeck's. But the dream must give way to the harsh reality, as Charlie's dream did. Neither George nor Lennie knows this: Mr. Steinbeck keeps it from George—hence the catastrophe. Charlie and Paulette hit the road again—still together, still romantic, still in love. That's something. But what has George got after he has disposed of Lennie? His real problem is just beginning. He can't go out and begin knocking large, useful males on the knob. What will he be?— the truth is breathtaking: an itinerant worker with an unrealizable dream, but a dream which has become a historic myth: a creator has murdered his creation because it didn't work. No, not even though it should have been patented in Washington! It just isn't in nature. Too bad, George, try again. But first, be stronger than your creator, John Steinbeck. Dispose of *him!* There are other, better dreams.

It would be refreshing to think that Hollywood had neatly counterposed in rival studios Mickey, the mechanical principle of joy, and Lennie, the mechanical principle of horror. But it was not to be. Mr. Disney made his first error when he went in for a certain "humanization" of his artificial dynamic of action. When I saw *Snow White and the Seven Dwarfs*, I was disturbed by the movements of Snow White and the Prince in the earlier sequences, and then I realized that Mr. Disney had actually effected an approximation of the cinematic principle of human movement. Publicity on the picture had already revealed that the animated drawings were copied after movies of an actor and actress impersonating the cartoon characters. So much for "scientific" efficiency! Instead of economy and the illusion of extra speed and grace, absolutely essential to the generic success of animated cartoons, one got in Snow White and the Prince a pastiche of ease and awkwardness: a *redundance* of mechanical movements; actually, a reversion to nickelodeon cinema. Again the apotheosis of American esthetic intelligence, which had broken into the dumping-ground of artistic megalomania. Mr. Disney could not stop there . . . He did not stop there . . .

The rôle of music in the animated cartoons has always been an integral one. Jazz was especially apt—and Toscanini is known to have praised a Disney pictorial interpretation of the *William Tell* Overture. I wonder what Toscanini thinks of *Fantasia* . . . Music, so often compared with mathematics, assuredly has the appearance of obeying inexorable laws. Counterpoint and dissonance, typical modern devices, have been most helpful in the effects of animated cartoons. At any rate, it is apparent that the movement of animated cartoons tends toward the ultimate synthesis of *movements* as music tends toward the ultimate synthesis of *sounds*. When Mr. Disney conceived *Fantasia*, he evidently had some such thing in mind, for he chose certain classic examples of music and correlated with their orthodox rendition practically his whole troupe of animated creations, his whole repertoire of effects. As Tschaikovsky and Wagner gave all they had, he wished to give all he had. In this sense so morally satisfying, this formula in the same sense is esthetically catastrophic. For now Mr. Disney was what he was not very definitely before: an illustrator; and being a man of distinction, an illustrator with an aggressive sense of interpretation.

What is the sight-seer and the sound-hearer to make of *Fantasia?* Why were these culturally disparate things put together? What is in the music that could be interpreted by Mr. Disney's idiosyncratic sense of form? It must be understood that his talent as an artist is secondary to the type of movement given his forms: his art is specifically form-in-movement. Thus he has given us "comic" ballet in *Fantasia*, and also a "ballet" of impressionist forms. But his ballet is not really comic, any more than his forms are really impressionistic. By using the music of serious ballet, he is apparently parodying the ballet. Now the serious ballet may be parodied, as indeed it was recently by an American company, but special music was written for it; you can only parody the way a work of art has been done or the way it is now received. How can Mr. Disney parody the ballet with serious ballet music? What is he really poking fun at? All right, he is parodying the human. But why ballet? Why classical music? Whether he knows it or not, he is parodying the musical appreciation of the audience. His unconscious psychology is perfect, and he has actually projected on the screen in visual terms the aural responses of certain listeners to serious music. Those elephant and ostrich ballerinas are not mere optical witticisms, they represent many a listener doing the Dance of the Hours in his or her head. Therefore, seen from within, at the heart of its esthetic meaning, *Fantasia* is not a fantasy at all, but a most prosaic and sober sermon on the lagging wits of man, a blackboard illustration in psychological dynamics. Mickey Mouse and the others are ominous, they are independent of their creator, Walt Disney. With their subtle insouciance, they have trapped him into making a Frankenstein of music, which becomes a sublime and serious art interpreted from within by irresponsibly mechanized beasts. Are they not fully as irresponsible as those gaudy versions of science which appear in Hearst newspaper weeklies—dinosaurs which are but pen-and-ink animations of those re-created for natural history museums? In the case of *Fantasia*, their revivification becomes an incongruous invasion of music by popular science, a rape of spiritual profundity by the listener who dons the guise of music as awkwardly as Frankenstein donned the guise of the human body . . . Even an ichthyosaur becomes a mouse when music is a mousetrap.

CHAPTER VII

ORPHEUS A LA HOLLYWOOD

1. *The Geni from the Music Box*

In Chapter II, I have referred to the "totalizing" effect of music in the films—the need for musical accompaniment to re-create the effect of reality that was missing from silent pictures. But sound-recording came; pictures then supplied their own music, coinciding precisely with the action and supplementing it with sound effects to step-up reality; finally, the voice itself appeared, first in sequences and then throughout. Yet because the voice arrived, music was not relieved of its job. It was still required as a sort of vocal apparatus of destiny, a "chorus" to impress the spectator with the inner quality of the action by audibly sympathizing with it. Consequently *musical accompaniment* has the same place with reference to the modern movie as the chorus has to the ancient Greek theater. Four forms of contemporary theater exist in which music has an integrated rôle—the musical revue, the operetta, grand opera, and dance (ballet or native) as a spectacle separate from the revue. Hollywood has wisely neglected the third, but has been prolific in the first two. Indeed, the movie medium is peculiarly suited to run a gamut from straight operetta to regular movie plots with occasional songs. It has produced a voluminous array through romantic musicals, such as *Rose Marie, The Vagabond King,* and *Naughty Marietta,* to the musical extravaganzas of the *Follies* type interwoven with an "off-stage" plot. At this date, the gamut is very subtle. Nowhere is Hollywood so much at home as among gags, music, girls, and slapstick action: a mixture over which Manhattan reviewers gloat contemptuously with especial acidity toward the absence of "plot." But "plot" should not be too rudimentarily conceived. As to the literary element, Hollywood plots (as emphasized in Chapter I) are notably lacking in thorough structure, but the plot structure of a play is not necessarily the straight dramatic convention. Naïve reviewers speak of emptiness or illogicality of plot when emptiness and even "illogicality" have point, namely in musicals. Previously I referred only to the straight dramatic convention and its Hollywood handling. But the musical comedy convention, like grand opera, in bringing musical accompaniment into the theatrical medium and making it integral with the proceedings, makes it *part of the plot*. Thus a musical is Hollywood's truest "play" in the plot sense, not only because it is comic, but because it is musical—that is to say, *lyrical* rather than *dramatic*. Grand opera combines the lyric and the drama, elides the Greek play and the Greek Chorus. Even so, it is only comic grand opera, such as Mozart's *Marriage of Figaro*, that utterly succeeds as an artistic medium on the stage. Rossini, Verdi, Wagner —these opera composers, when presented in the theater, seem to satisfy less than they do as straight composers, when their music is performed purely orchestrally . . . for a reason which applies equally to presentation in the musical medium by Hollywood. It is much more difficult for the artifice of singing to "get across" in the tragic genre. The Greek and Shakespearean conventions of tragic drama seem more artistic; their artifices are the right ones for tragic feeling, of which poetic speech is the proper vocal medium. The "musical" and the "dramatic" can mix only when both make compromises—when the romantic comedy is essayed. Who can prefer *Tristan and Isolde* to *Figaro*, *Carmen* to *The Barber of Seville?* Only those who prefer symphonic music to theatre, or whose taste in opera is vulgar.

The special joy of the musical revue or romance is lyrical. The comedy convention absorbs song naturally, since song is celebrative rather than sacrificial—

when it is specifically *elegiac*, it becomes the chant, approaches the Greek Chorus and the lyric poem. Yet how would Hollywood be expected to judge properly even that convention it uses most intelligently? A good thing to Hollywood is a good thing, barring no circumstances. The real excuse for reviewers who chide music-and-gag movies for triteness or emptiness of plot is that, being Hollywood-educated, they have been hopelessly confused. Again, it is purely a question of a recipe so flexible that anything may be admitted so long as it adds "zest" to the dish. Sometimes the gags are not so good, the situations are tagged, the actors are overfamiliar or mediocre. Grounds for spectator complaint, assuredly. Oh, for a freshly-worked gag, or for a new prat-fall!—a prayer which was answered by Dietrich, who took several of them in *Destry Rides Again*. Not only must the Hollywood hoydens be mussed up but also the Hollywood ladies, and, the moment this is happening, the hoydens are being groomed for glamor parts in which not a hair of their heads will be disturbed. In the movie city, the "mortal" must eventually become the "divine," and vice versa. Thus, too, with music . . .

It must cease to be music, precisely, and become an embellishment of anything it accompanies. In the old days when serials were the rage, piano music served really onomatopoeic ends. It provided an extension of horses' hoofs and locomotive wheels, it

was the "crooning" of the lover's blood when he made
love to his sweetheart. Thus it was a *slavish* chorus,
not a philosophic commentary, not a semi-independ-
ent actor, as sometimes in Greek plays. It did not
illustrate a related but separate principle: it merely
echoed, reflected. It still does. For the best modern
cinema dramas and melodramas, special musical
arrangements are made or original scores written for
the incidental effects or orchestral accompaniment.
Often, we can forget their presence insofar as they
become automatically accepted conventions—like
operatic gestures. But in the case of *singing*, the
voice, an instrument of the actor, is also being *musical;* the convention is not only in the orchestra pit, it
is also on the stage. Thus music is in the integument
of the play as lyric poetry, in the person of the
Chorus in the Greek play, was in the integument of
the play. Only in the musical comedy and the operetta is this true of Hollywood procedure. Hollywood
does know a good thing, but it can never control it.
It has allowed music ostentatiously to visit plots into
which it does not properly fit, or fits only according to
a certain "naturalistic" convention which I shall proceed to illustrate.

Like everything else in the movie city, music is
filled with its own importance to an overweening degree. The chief example of Hollywood's musical
"opportunism" is a kind of biography of the young

singing star—Deanna Durbin being the outstanding, yet by no means the only, example. These films have a dominant motif: the power of a young female voice (always aspiring to operatic stature) to stop traffic, hypnotize all males in listening distance, and otherwise take charge of planetary affairs. It is the wish-fulfillment myth of the music in the pit to become part of the play; its voice is young, it has a success story on its lips. Miss Durbin's voice caresses the microphone and out leaps the Geni of Grand Opera. At the worst, she may be expected to become a Jeanette MacDonald. The Svengalian eye of the movie camera looks at a young girl and Trilbyizes her; it does no less to a mythical music score for a Hollywood drama—that music score which subconsciously, one feels, wants the heroine to be a Jeanette Mac-Donald, even if she is really a Norma Shearer. "Why can't all actresses *sing?*" the music seems to ask.

A type of singing dramatic actress does exist, such as Irene Dunne. This type occasionally takes the part of an opera star (indeed, the opera stars, Lily Pons, Grace Moore, and Gladys Swarthout, have all enacted "themselves" in Hollywood). The fundamental pattern, even for the revue singing star, is always the success story, with the picture seldom covering a sufficient span to include degeneration of career. But an actress such as Miss Dunne is not likely to be adrift, even if she parts from her movie career, for she is not only wedded to dramatic acting and singing, but also, I believe, to vaudeville, in which she once played, just as Joan Crawford used to dance in revues. Like many movie actresses, Miss Dunne has a versatile repertory from straight to character to singing to comedy. Even if pride should not permit actresses to step down a few pegs, they can always console themselves, if they ultimately prefer obscurity, with thinking, "I could go back to the old stuff if I wanted to."

This multiple professional personality has a parallel in the technical virtuosity of music and its Hollywood rôles. A spectacular song or music-and-dance sequence can appear in the very middle of a Hollywood comedy romance (take Fred Astaire's films), occupy from five to ten minutes, and then allow the "plot" to proceed. In the case of Mr. Astaire, the naturalistic convention of the dancer's climb to fame replaces that of the singer. This particular genre illustrates perhaps better than any other what I mean by the *plot* as *charade*. The only purpose of the Durbin and Astaire "plots" is to reveal their respective and true professions: dance and song. By this token, plot becomes a relatively artificial convention while, at the same time, it is apparently realistic. The Durbin-Astaire myth pattern is simply at the top of the hierarchy of Hollywood's musical opportunism. But it is nevertheless a patent indication of Hollywood's conspiracy to use music as a highly plastic substructure of "plot" in order to bolster its esthetic irresponsibility. Hollywood is dedicated to exposing the common esthetic rôle of music as a public pacifier, a crowd consoler, a decorative deceiver. Thus, its uses of music are intended to supply a "harmony" obviously missing from real experience, and which must be missing from it, since music is but a *symbol* of moral harmony and cannot convert reality into harmony, either magically by appearing like a geni or by faithfully following the plot around like a bodyguard. The ideal effect of the success story of the girl singer would be to convince the world that reality (if caught young enough) may become glamorous and beautiful and that, provided sufficient push is applied, "she" may even be married. And even if you don't marry her, she can, like Jeanette MacDonald, be watched and heard, if that much will satiate you.

2. *The Poetry Cure for the Castration Complex*

It was obviously with music as the "naturalistic convention," rather than as pure artifice that Hollywood would offend the most inartistically; and therefore it is not surprising that music should unaccountably take the form, in this instance, of what is perhaps Hollywood-conceived as the most ambiguous and irresponsible of dulcet mellifluities: poetry. A very recent film, *King's Row*, is a grim sort of opposite to anything that might actually suggest a "musical" happiness. It tells of a community askew, an American town in the last century which is very conscious of the differences existing on either side of the railroad track. On one side is Robert Cummings (heavily made up) and Respectability (likewise heavily made up), and on the other side are the Ross girls, heavily made up in one way but, alas, lightly made up in another. All is not hotsy-totsy on the right side of the old town—you can bet the Judith Anderson in your home on that. For *King's Row* is one of those "revolutionary" Hollywood products which bear down with no end of phony pressure on supposedly "nice" people. It is the *wrong* side of the railroad track that gets away without murder. There are bats in the belfries of the nice people for the logical reason that it is they who own the belfries, or their equivalents, whereas the Ross "chippies" can afford nothing more dangerous to the soul than canaries in cages.

A "nice" young girl goes inconspicuously insane and is murdered by her "nice" father, who then commits suicide. Betty Field has been chosen to die in this way, but Ann Sheridan has been elected to live in quite another. She is the humble sweetheart of a young man whose legs are cut off by a surgeon having an uncontrollable but wholly unscientific passion for cruelty. Guilty of a delusion of grandeur, the surgeon despises the town's well-bred "sinners" and wreaks his private brand of punishment on them whenever there is a minor accident. This sadist is taken by Hollywood in perfect stride, and appropriate music is found for him. Why not? The look-the-other-way toleration of certain residents of King's Row has permitted his peculiar practice to continue; accordingly, sadism has its moral "music," its conciliating principle in the "respectable" part of society, its god from the juke-box of the hidden soul. Just as certain circles of society feel that "snubbing" is the most cruel fate that can be dealt anyone or anything, Hollywood has ritually "snubbed" reality. But Hollywood tries to make up for such "inhumanities" in its own manner.

The real crisis in the film develops when the young man without the legs, even though certain of the devotion of the girl he loves and marries, acquires an inferiority complex. Dr. Cummings, who has become a psychiatrist, undertakes his cure, but is really stumped when, learning that the legs have been *needlessly* amputated, he fears that this information might undermine his patient's mental cure at one blow. The crying—or should I say singing?—need of therapeutic harmony is obvious in the case of this plot. Since it is drama, however, music can hardly be dragged in by Dr. Stokowski's coattails. Thus, it is hopelessly confined to the artificial convention of the orchestral accompaniment, and the play, needing the naturalistic convention of music (or its equivalent) is in a pickle. Robert Cummings is not Nelson Eddy, nor is Nelson Eddy Ronald Reagan, the young man who has been victimized by the mad surgeon. Mr. Eddy, obviously, would sing himself out of any dungeon, even the Dungeon of Despair.

I do not exaggerate: the manipulation of the plot, as it turns out, is visibly and audibly on my side. I am ignorant of whether such a device of musical magic occurs in the original story; all I know in this case is what I witnessed in the movie theater. The concrete and dialectical presence of some intense sweet strains from the Orphic realm was deemed so badly needed by the music doctors in the studio that application was made (if the suggestion was not already in the story) to the sibylline science of poetry. It must be explained that Dr. Cummings has a genuinely difficult problem on his hands, because the mad surgeon (now dead) has left a sexually frustrated daughter who can relieve her distraught mind only by telling of her father's crimes. And the first one she wants to tell, rather inevitably, is her ex-suitor, the young man with the inferiority complex—or, as I am inclined to believe, the castration complex. Be this as it may, the young woman is temporarily dissuaded from her purpose, though Dr. Cummings realizes that his patient is by no means safe from her. Then romance lures the young doctor away from his duty. He is willing, after meeting a charming young woman, to chuck the cure and elope to Vienna where he has a psychiatrist's post, leaving the legless youth at the mercy of the tale-teller. While his intended consents to the elopement, she implies that she would not be proud to go. In this dilemma, the young doctor arrives at an instant and brilliant decision: he'll break the news himself so that it will not matter if the deranged female Winchell finally does get to the microphone. Of course, he's taking a big chance in switching his methods in this manner, since apparently he does not at once realize the advanced stage of Hollywood's musical thera-peutics. You feel as though, seeing Dr. Cummings break at the barrier, he might not get to the patient's bedside first. But he does, and asking him to hold out his jaw, since he's about to take it, Dr. Cummings delivers a remarkable "left," the bad news, but not without preceding it with an even more remarkable "right" from that famous fistic manual, *The Oxford Book of English Verse*; the poem is Henley's "In-victus." This pugilistically-read psychiatrist, appearing with a poem on his lips, has all the effect of a *deus ex machina*. Of course, he is really the geni from the music box, with whom Miss Durbin is on such ex-cellent terms, and thus should not astonish us too much. Anyway, the patient is saved. And if the patient is saved, the method is vindicated. Yet as a paying customer, I reserve the right to derive my own reaction of the macabre from this movie. I recall that a geni comes from the East, which is also the home of a character praised by Kipling. Assuredly, now, the ghost of Freud can address the ghost of the poet: "You're a better man than I am, Dr. Kipling."

CHAPTER VIII

JOHN DOE; OR, THE FALSE ENDING

IN THE beginning is the end. This purely formal myth had had an uncomputable amount of popularity long before the invention of the movie camera. "Fate" is one of the terms it has been known by, and, in Greek drama, it took the form of an inescapable trap for the hero, laid by the gods especially to be his undoing. No matter how clever a tragic hero may be (Macbeth is the classic example of the precautionary hero of tragedy), he winds up in the toils which apparently are his own creation but which, supernaturalists would have us believe, have been merely a thought that has occurred to an Omnipotent Being or Beings. In other chapters I have shown the Hollywood conception of fate rather indirectly in relation to the villain and the hero, but here I will examine *the plot* as an overall element, an "omnipotent" conception which business acumen has lodged firmly in the minds of the cinema

city, from the industry's owners to the script writers
and film editors. The movie makers are virtually the
gods of Hollywood, and the actors and actresses, the
divine impersonations, are the contemporary vestiges
of that Old Omnipotence of love, war, wisdom, and
nature which was Greece's.

At the top of the hierarchy of Greek society were
the gods. We may consider it a hierarchy because the
gods, like men, had names, homes, and families as
well as specified "political" duties. Moreover, they
were individuals in a sense which the Hebrew-Chris-
tian hierarchy (aside from Christ Himself) were not;
that is, in polytheism there is a chance for individual
insistence and expansion, as well as for such a thing
as filial rebellion, whereas, we know very well, the mono-
theist Christ is the Obedient Son of the history of religion. The caste nature of pagan society permitted the
exclusivism of the gods, whose visits to the earth were
purely occasional, and not missionary as was Christ's.
But although the caste feeling of pagan divinity was
static, there were assumed to be internal quarrels, and
so *human* quarrels were simply a reproduction on a
lower moral level of the dissidence that perpetually occurred in divine society; moreover, the gods contended
with each other in influencing the fates of mortals. In
this way there was a type of demarcated internal freedom in all pagan society; and if the gods ruled the
destinies of individuals it was only, as we learn from

Greek myths and dramas, because they took a personal interest in certain individuals. There was no assumption as in Christian mythology that God and the angels perpetually watch over the destinies of all human beings.

Greek democracy was a democracy of castes and of a particular nation. But Christ appeared as the first planetary democrat, and as the first indication that divine nature has an unconscious wish to fuse itself with human nature, namely, to intervene in such a way that no human being can ever forget his own divinity. Such was the ideal; the reality is self-evident. In Christian monotheism, direct intervention in human affairs by the divine nature automatically equalized the access which each individual had to God's audience. Which is to say, while it was not practically demonstrable that "God dwells in every man," it could be ideally assumed—but since, as a constant fact, it could be *only* ideally assumed, God had to continue His heavenly residence and supervise the divine course of human events from that remoteness. Once having sent His Only Son, and thus imitated the human duress of losing Him, God had provided an object lesson for the planet: a supreme illustration of humility. As Christianity spread westward, it met paganism, and paganism dialectically transformed it into the Church; namely, a permanent symbolic visit by divine nature through a highly organized human iconography. It is not the blood of a beast or a man, but the "blood of Christ," which is sacrificed in the Catholic ritual! Hence the lack of distinction made by the participant in the ritual between the actual "blood" drunk and the blood of Christ is testimony to the extreme urgency of the permanent symbolic residence of the divine on earth. In practice, of course, the Catholic Church was created by the priest caste purely as a political weapon against the State: the inevitable result of the democratization and terrestrialization of the divine . . . Am I far afield from Hollywood? Not at all. For what happened universally to the fatal plot of drama and myth? Hollywood, which excludes nothing necessarily, inherited this consequence of Christianity . . . It is known as the Happy Ending.

To begin with, it is not death. Nor is it disgrace, unless disgrace is repaid by death, as the criminal pays for his evil happiness in the electric chair. It is often symbolic death, however, the beginning of redemption, of a "new life." This last term rings familiarly. Did not Christ die to redeem human sin? Did His death not precede resurrection? The agony on the Cross was only the end of the beginning. The beginning of the end is . . . Easter: promises, optimism. Yet life, of course, is what happens between the beginning and the end, between birth and death, between Hollywood and the movie public. It is the between in which art, no matter what its periodic endings, is permanently interested, namely, in the means by which all ends are attained, all beginnings propelled. Only a proper conception of the reality of the between, however, can avail either an important ending or a significant beginning. The conduct of life *as an idea* is the essence of morality, and opposed to the maybe of morality is the fatal symmetry of the beginning-indistinguishable-from-the-end, one reciprocally being implied in the other. This symmetry can exist, however, only under certain conditions of control over human morality, over terrestrial conduct. That is, a control from above: a control by supernature. Art is an imitation of life *only if* the conditions of life are fatally conceived by the creative artist—if he understands the pattern perceived in nature as the operation of a law imposed by an Omnipotent Being. If the artist, man, becomes the "omnipotent" being, plot no longer possesses this fluid ambivalence between beginning and end. In romantic fiction and the modern novel and drama, the artist has assumed this omnipotence, and hence his plots are notably "unfatalistic." For instance, in Ibsen, Shaw, and Pirandello, the characters in one way or another debate among themselves what the end shall be. To preserve the classic conception of fate, James Joyce had to parody a classic plot or, as in *Finnegans Wake*, make the cyclic pattern of the mind the only fatal design in living. Joyce and Proust have this in common; their chief plots are merely manifestations of the desire to repeat mechanically, to rehearse faithfully what has happened to them or their friends. Hence the beginning of Proust's novel is also the end only because the mind is assumed to be instinctively cyclic and its mode a series of unchangeable mechanical links. The causation of supposed fictitious events is taken to be psycho-physical, and limited in Proust's case absolutely by personal experience. Both the "I" of Proust's novel and Finnegan are heroes who, psychologically considered, are always in bed, always passive, always lying on their backs with springs of apprehension coiled to surprise the black curtain of night or memory when it shall burst into a cinematic brilliance of image and movement. All that Proust knows of events is what did happen, nothing of what might have happened . . . an alternative which has been avidly seized by Hollywood and the Christian Scientists. Of course, I do not mean that Proust literally reproduced events. We know he did not, but he invented the closest possible analogies to events within the realm of discretion, and left the logical, causational pattern the same.

Naturally, that a certain fate or necessity exists in human behavior is not universally denied by modernity any more than by antiquity. But in the absence of a controlling factor from "above," or at least, definitely outside the human being, the "necessity" becomes inner, and thus involved with the pure instincts of man, the activities of the various layers of his civi-lized-animal nature. It is thus inevitable that a romantic view of this situation should more or less alternate with a realistic or naturalistic view in artistic periods. There arose, as a result, the school of naturalist fiction, in which a primitive, environmental necessity reigns over human acts. It was logical that Hollywood, as a sort of esthetic "opium of the people" and the folk art of the cities, should tend toward a romantic view of neces-sity, of the causal factor of plot. In a previous chapter, I have discussed the romantic adventure film as a genre, and as its sub-genre, the film glorifying the gangster. Moral choices by the heroes of such films are cut to a crude conventional pattern, and so they are actuated by motives whose ambiguous good-evil character is not confusing on the surface, nor complex. This is because, giving themselves to a forthright kind of action, these heroes are caught up instantly within the *legal plot*, that is, within the ever-present toils of local fiats and taboos. Such "fatality," however, is purely delimiting, since it is statically opposed to in-dividual excess and exotic desires, possessing a rigidity which not even the most hardened criminal is disposed to quarrel with in theory. Such good villains as the gangster and the romantic adventurer primarily set out to release themselves systematically from social obligation, but not to modify the theory on which the laws of society are based; they are *escapist*. On the other hand, the nature of the tragic hero is that he is superhuman. He has the god-delusion, and believes that by his own genius he can change the nature of fate, overcome whatever "omnipotence" there be. We see very well the pass to which the tragic hero has come in Hollywood; he is *Superman*, who has succeeded, by the grace of comic-strip humor, in transcending the psychic, neural, and physical limitations which hitherto have fatally bound the behavior of the individual. Thus, he is a sort of substitute imagined by a Christian Science esthete; as a result, his *métier* is not moral tragedy but romantic comedy.

And yet the average Hollywood hero is by no means a superman. He veers from the romantic-realistic hero of Tyrone Power to the romantic-realistic hero of Gary Cooper, with such drawing-room types as George Brent, Fredric March, and William Powell to impersonate the buccaneers of "parlor, bedroom, and bath." The plexuses of action in which all these men are involved might be termed the Domestic Tangle, the Military or Soldier of Empire Tangle, the Criminal Tangle, the Pioneer or Soldier of Fortune Tangle, and the Civil Ambition Tangle, representing the fields of home, war, gangsterism, travel, and business. All these spheres roughly indicate, either by themselves or their casual interlacings, the limits of various plot-patterns. Though Hollywood stood up faithfully to the task of doing a rather flat version of Dreiser's *American*

Tragedy, it is usually thoroughly inept in the genre of naturalistic tragedy, as in the actually fantastic *Of Mice and Men*. In any case, Dreiser's conception was a much-inflated pathological study, rendered almost opaque by a quaint variety of humanitarianism.

No matter what the plot-pattern or the hero type, Hollywood movies notably tend to begin with a bang and end with a whimper, a sigh, or a grin. The faithful diagnostician of the movies sometimes complains that this or that picture begins so well and ends so poorly. This conclusion is often esthetically sound as far as it goes, but it holds only a beginning for criticism. Among the more sophisticated patrons, it is resignedly accepted as a convention that the ending of a picture is pretty unimportant. Indeed? Why do the patrons permit themselves this passive, laissez-faire sophistication? Apparently because it is enough only to have glimpsed the gods quarreling, semi-nude, in the same predicament as us poor mortals! Indeed, so far as many patrons go, that is the underlying answer to the question. But do the Hollywood gods and goddesses take a personal interest in mortals, as did their proto-types in Ancient Greece? They do not. One of their main problems is to prevent our taking too personal an interest in them—and well they might, for it is they who have done more to break down the conceptual distinction between publicity and privacy than any other element in modern democratic life. On the contrary their private lives are subject to our indirect, mass intervention, and therefore they are compelled, assisted considerably by their press agents, to keep their lives in normal working order with a decent minimum of scandals and divorces.

But where is the origin of authority, in their myth sphere or ours? Which follows the lead? This question is like that of which came first, the chicken or the egg, and can be applied to the theme of the present chapter. Logically, it makes little difference as a rule whether the end of a Hollywood movie should be at the beginning or the end, because both start and climax are *premature*. To art, it is the fate of the grown "chicken" that matters. What interferes with this interest of Hollywood in the "chicken's" mature fate is that its conception of entertainment is merely to watch it lay an egg—watch things happen without maintaining the integrity of the causal pattern. When *reality* and *entertainment* are thus held identical, all endings are purely conventional, formal, and often, like the charade, of an infantile logic. "Ah," you may say, "but Hollywood is healthy; it has the sense of life, it is not interested in endings, for endings imply death; let death come casually—yes, even mechanically, and with little 'reality.' Let life somehow seem to go on." (Resurrection, Easter promises, and so on.) Personally, I can see no merit in this conception of the vitality of Hollywood, excepting that it indirectly provides an excellent preparation for the selfless sacrifice of the soldier's life in warfare. What matter the time of death, or its manner, so long as one has lived, so long as others shall live? The influence of Hollywood is not to be discounted in such considerations. But I must confine myself primarily to esthetic values. I am engaged in showing what Hollywood is as a manufacturer of hallucinations.

Two recent movies occur to me as striking and strikingly contrasting examples of the "false ending," which is my term for Hollywood's happy ending. It is not merely that the conclusions of the action in these pictures are unsatisfying or ridiculous, but also because they are but the logical results of a pristine confusion of purposes and slandering of reality. *Suspicion*, so streamlined on the surface, is a mesh of fictional incongruities. The story is a melodramatic thriller the original basis of which as a book may well be dubious. First, it seems likely that only an unattractive young spinster would have fallen so hard for an obvious society adventurer such as Cary Grant portrays, and then have felt justified in suspecting him of a desire to murder her for her money. Joan Fontaine, who plays the woman, is a handsome young person, but let us assume that she could indeed, being so attractive, suddenly have realized her true sexual longings only when Mr. Grant appeared. Of course,

on the screen, Miss Fontaine's heroine shows no sign
of that complex due to suppressed sexuality which
one would expect to motivate such a bold romantic
gesture as her marriage with the high-stepping Mr.
Grant's hero. I understand that in the original story
the husband does murder the wife, and thus her
suspicions are justified. If, I say, we accept this conclusion for the plot, then we have to deal with many
things as *beginnings* which Hollywood does not
allow. Consequently, it was only natural that, visualiz-
ing a happy ending, Hollywood would consistently
prepare for it by adapting the material. Thus, Mr.
Grant is his usual self, not at all implying he might
murder somebody, much less his own wife, and Miss
Fontaine is also herself, and not at all the morbid and
unattractive type she could more plausibly have been.
Given the original plot (that he eventually murders
her), there is but one reasonably possible hypothesis:
that a very clever and completely unscrupulous adventurer systematically victimizes an ugly, naïve, sex-
starved spinster; because a beautiful woman would be
murdered by her husband only out of passion, either
of sadism or revenge, but then he would never be the
petty fraud Mr. Grant's hero is. On the contrary, given
the events of the movie plot (that the wife's suspicions
are a misunderstanding), there is but one reasonably
possible hypothesis,which the movies do not assume:
the creation of her suspicion is due to the absence of

sexual satisfaction—a deduction which is only elementary.

Hollywood, however, always has its own logic, and this is that, considering the events of the plot taken together with the characters, Mr. Grant could not have murdered Miss Fontaine. But then the spectator has to assume that her suspicions are hallucinatory and thus require a pathological basis. It is true that the couple are acquainted with a detective-story writer, and at dinner the subject of murder and its detection and method is discussed. This creates an opportunity for the wife's suspicion to gain head, but a fresh opportunity does not account for the basic situation, for which a pre-existing emotion is necessary. Well, there *is* one of a sort: Mr. Grant has been a financial finagler and petty deceiver, a fact which the wife has soon discovered, but knowing that her husband does not have the conventional sense of honor is far from imagining he desires to murder her. Indeed, his lack of conventional ethics is only too commonplace and explicable on social grounds of an obvious nature, and if the shock were too great, she could have gone home to mother at once. But she stays on. Thus, the psychological link between impatience and shame at her husband's unstable morality and suspicion that he wants to murder her—this necessary link is missing from the evidence. Where is it? Unfortunately, Hollywood as yet has imported it very gingerly; it is the sexual neurosis. Only the husband's social behavior combined with his sexual behavior could have adduced emotional hallucination on top of moral shock. At one point in the crisis, the wife denies the husband her bedroom. This is very strange, unless we assume that she is either frigid and has grown to find sex repulsive, or that she is using her suspicion as a device to excuse her husband at night from that which he cannot successfully accomplish. Understanding this as the reality, the climax of the film, which pictures Mr. Grant's heroically taking the desperate situation in hand and promising to reform is merely a hoax, an element of charade. Because nothing has happened powerful enough to induce him to be different. He has not even learned the cause of his wife's nervousness; even assuming that he suddenly understands, as the picture wants us to assume, that some hysterical fear possesses his wife, and that this is enough to convince him he has been cruel and selfish, the real situation, as the movie ends, is just beginning! What has happened? Hollywood has indulged in a little charade (titled, you will notice, with the three-syllable word, *Suspicion*) in order to disclose the possibility of a real dramatic struggle between husband and wife. One has the terrible "suspicion" that if the camera remained on the scene, one would be treated to endless quarrels between the wife and husband as to who is right and who is wrong, and then only things would be said which have already been said by Bernard Shaw. But at least most of the cards would be face up on the table. Neurotic domestic relations would be portrayed as something of what they are. But Hollywood's wisdom is profitable if not profound. Of the consequences of such a sexual situation, once it is apt to become thoroughly visible between husband and wife, Hollywood creates its own brand of comedy drama . . . but that would be in another picture and at another admission price.

For instance: *Meet John Doe*. I could not help thinking, as I gazed at Gary Cooper's face, that the most serious commonplace hero of the century in art, Joyce's H. C. Earwicker (H.C.E. or Here Comes Everybody) presents a weird antithesis to the hero of this film. The essence of Earwicker's commonplaceness is contained in the night, in dreams, in passivity, in the anonymity of the last layer of the libido as it stands, stark and abstract, in the starless universe of sleep. Alas, the hero is literally on his back! But instead of kicking him when he is down, as the world wants to do to John Doe, Joyce devises a subtle, sadomasochistic scheme to elevate Earwicker to a linguistic paradise: the beyond-which-not of the psychic monologue, the stream of consciousness which is unconsciousness. John Doe, however, is not a pampered literary figment of this kind. He is an ordinary man, make no mistake, and because Mr. Cooper has the certain charm he was born with, his ordinariness appears as human goodness, human benevolence, human enthusiasm for the human race.

Oh, boy! Some picture! Here Comes Everybody out of bed and on his feet and in the political race. Then: *Horrors!* The Frankenstein of fascism looms in the poor fellow's bathroom mirror. He's been duped. And by the girl he thought was wonderful. He's just been *used.* Ideals don't mean a thing to his backers. In fact, he's been a mere figurehead in a wicked plot to hoodwink and bulldoze the public . . . *his* public: all those John Does out there . . . and listen—*those are boos* . . . Well, if they want a fight, here's a fight, and John Doe plunges into the melee. He also sees that the public is unhoodwinked and then—is tempted to throw himself off the Empire State Building, going so far as the railing on the observation tower. Here was a neat little thesis on the dangers of believing in a political upstart, because he may be the cat's paw of crooked interests—a covert warning against the fascistic Huey Longs, as well as a choice fable on the pathos of the average man's benevolent instincts and gross credulity.

The chivalry of the average American is exploited to its peace-time (pre-war) maximum by making capital of his impulse to crusade for politics that will right all social and economic evils, and so on. But the most important thing the movie does is to admit the existence of a large audience for the individual crusading fervor of a Coughlin or a Long—and this audience is no less than all the John Does out there, who also, sensing something has been imported from Denmark, desire rather helplessly to do something about it.

This is the common or garden variety of the messianic complex in all the nakedness of its provincial panoply. Here the Hollywood hero-god steps down from his heaven and strips off the theatrical mask (this is easy for Mr. Cooper, who apparently wears the simplest make-up) and says to John Doe: "Look, I'm you after all. I'm really that fellow in the bathroom mirror. But because I am also an instrument of divine power, I shall intervene in your affairs to your advantage. Accept me, and the Kingdom of Heaven on Earth will be yours." But this, as an *ending*, would not be realistic enough—it would not correspond to the actual experience of John Doe, who, being a wage-earner, is a realist during his waking hours. Therefore the hero-god-actor must admit he is merely an impersonator, merely acting in a charade, really Gary Cooper, not John Doe or Huey Long . . . Thus, his suicide, whether consummated in the movie or not, is inherent in the pattern; it constitutes a symbolic change of identity from the picture's John Doe to Hollywood's John Doe (né Gary Cooper). Consequently, the ending is *the death of the hero*, whether Hollywood has elected he shall die or be restored alive to the arms of the heroine . . . Of course, Hollywood insists on the Resurrection and the Redemption; hence, in the conclusion that was finally decided on, Mr. Cooper leaves the building by going down in the elevator, and he and Miss Stanwyck decide to work patiently and without illusions for the "end" which has been missed in the film: the political salvation of the American nation and perhaps even the human race.

The end has become the beginning in the sense of "If at first you don't succeed . . ." Actually, there is no cosmic fatality to the failure of an individual or of a single effort by a group or an individual to effect a social improvement. Yet Hollywood's artistic failure is fatal, because the individualistic moral terms are too ambiguous, the specific fable is oversimplified and thus mystifying. The film's mores are those of the *status quo*, and so *Meet John Doe* can easily be conceived as propaganda for human sacrifice of individual life in war—a war which is ostensibly fought for human ideals under the general classification of democracy. At this point in planetary affairs, American democracy becomes the theoretical right to hold a job and vote every four years for a new president. Thus, the war for democracy is strictly a struggle for preservation of the political and economic *status quo*. Consequently such a political fable, when it emanates from Hollywood, is constrained to impose *the political reality of democ-racy* as the only "fate" conceivable, the only "omnip-otent" plot from "above," able to determine the end for the hero.

As it was in the beginning for John Doe under Roosevelt, so shall it be in the end. And his real name can be O'Reilly or Ginsberg. According to Hollywood, the first and last letters of the alphabet of human hap-piness are A—and by this token, the twenty-four other letters are only A's in disguise. As for Z . . . On the other hand, there is nothing divine or insuperable in the political "plot." Political reality is fluid and alto-gether terrestrial: it likewise is a product of the civi-lized animal nature, and arises from social evolution. It is not immortal. In Shakespeare, a new king was usually crowned on the death site of his predecessor, thus insuring the continuation of the system. The Hollywood happy ending is false because it is pseudo-divine, just as the Hollywood fate is false because it is pseudo-tragic—and both depend upon an optimistic re-beginning. Christian Science, the "science" which converts hope of heaven into mundane optimism, is no more than a straight-faced burlesque of Christian-ity. The great fundamental esthetic of Hollywood is a perversion of the sound Aristophanic principle of a burlesque of the gods; Hollywood's is a *straight-faced* burlesque of the gods. Notice that in America you can be satirical about anything but religion, the divine aspect. It is exempted in the social pact made with the heterogeneous elements of American democracy: Obey the political and economic laws, and you are free to worship as you please. By common consent, therefore, this is the sacred individual province, upon whose solemnity nobody but a hoodlum will trespass.

The Hollywood "gods" and "goddesses" raise all mundane traits to a humorlessly divine level, because as an impregnable group they seem to us rich, happy, carefree, and handsome or charming. A Jean Gabin or Charles Laughton may appear throughout a movie in dungarees or rags, it is only a professional masquerade; not only are they presumably "gentlemen of nature," but they are known to visit nightclubs outside of working hours; at the worst, they are dude ranchers, or they putter around yachts. Whatever they do of this kind, you may be sure it is a condescension, a "pleasure game," such as charades, barn dances, or kiddie-parties. By this logic, when they appear "ridiculously" poor, uneducated, or stupid on the screen, one ought to laugh as everyone does at kiddie-parties or the like. Yet one doesn't, simply because the Hollywood gods are themselves straight-faced, and we know they want us to be. If we weren't, they'd lose their contracts, and that would be "tragic." Such moral and esthetic values as beauty, virtue, and intellect are assumed to be so common and easily owned in the movies that they have a dizzying ambivalence. Like those signs reading "Applause" held up for the audience in radio studios, laughter-cues in the movies are implicit. Beauty and brains are neatly replaced by that peculiarly cynical, American, and compensatory humor which takes a "democratically" excusing view toward spiritual and mental defects. This comprises, in a sense, "legitimate" comedy. But Hollywood's emphasis is strictly indigenous. Ignorance of modern adult education is assumed in the audience and flattered. A word such as "psychiatry" is treated as hifalutin, and persons otherwise apparently educated are made to apologize to each other on the screen for using such a word by joking about it. A noticeably literary form of speech is ritually associated with mental infirmity—there springs to mind a rôle played by Claude Rains in *Moontide*, that of a water-front philosopher significantly nicknamed "Nutsy." Perhaps I myself seem mentally extravagant to cavil at such well-established devices on stage and screen. But if we compare the use of a "literary" sort of madness in Gorki's *The Lower Depths* (a French version) with that typical of American movies, we see that philosophers and actors, no less than clerks, are driven mad by poverty; thus, an inclination toward aphorism, poetry, and hallucination has a profoundly serious source, and its juxtaposition with poverty is compounded equally of tragedy and comedy. There have been a few contemporary efforts to portray the modern bohemian literary clown in the theater, but none has found its way whole into Hollywood.

Therefore, in line with the psychology of the movie city, only an intellectual crank or an obsessed esthete would demand an "inevitable" climax to a narrative. So Hollywood takes a markedly sophisticated view of "endings." Perhaps the deepest source of the esthetic of "false endings" is in the movie serial, which remains a symptom of Hollywood's early desire to set up a perpetual motion of human activity as "great adventure." Old and new serials possess both super-men and super-women, capable of endless effort and resistance. This is a beautiful myth. If only it were not so ideal!

CHAPTER IX

" . . . WHERE THE BODY LIES"

I have spoken at much length of the *inalienably* visible in Hollywood movies. In this manner, I have considered and made judgments of *the forms* which are characteristic, and also I have tried to show in various ways the limitation and perversion of the content as a result of formal errors or defects. The most crucial instance of the omission of form is in regard to the sexual behavior of Hollywood lovers, which I discussed in "The Technicolor of Love." This, as I believe I showed, exposed an evasion of a certain moral problem in sex: the significance of the Single Instance. There is, however, a "single instance" toward which Hollywood takes a totally inverted point of view; it is *murder*. This act is no less "secret" than that of sex, but in the obvious ethical interests of society, it is far more important to turn up the murderer than the fornicator. The fornicator, even if his act is immoral and

may lead to evil consequences, is engaged in life-giv-
ing, whereas the murderer is a life-taker.

I have provided here no treatment of the purely
technical aspects of cinema narrative, but it is obvious
that such narrative has peculiar problems and individual solutions; even though such solutions may resemble closely the narrative, both psychological and physical, of literature. The camera is devoted at all times
to telling its tale—excepting when a murder has been
committed or some criminal uncaught or unidentified,
and then it must close its eye out of sagacity. The
peculiar joy of the camera—and the best Hollywood
technicians have discovered how to handle this effect
—is to reveal . . . and to reveal often with an artless
open-eyedness, carrying with it at times a naïve kind
of coquetry. The art of introducing a character or a
theme or an incident is naturally advanced in all
branches of the arts, but, in the case of the movies, it
must be remembered that it is necessary to keep before the eye much that is not always intrinsically interesting in relation to the main narrative, a fact especially true of Hollywood, and the consequences of
which I indicated in "Hollywood's Surrealist Eye."
This is due not only to the vacuity of many Hollywood
themes, but also to the inelasticity of the camera when
its lack of absorbing material places upon its *distrac-
tion-value* an unusually heavy burden. There is one
stereotyped solution for inner vacuity in Hollywood,

and that, naturally, is outer activity: the show-offism of the camera; the sheer skill in presenting the most commonplace realities. Yet a time comes, as I have just hinted, when quite another problem of entertainment exists for the camera, a much more literary and psychological problem—a problem concerned crucially with the relation of form to content: the narration of the detection of crime.

Of course, the detective novel is itself an advanced form, and it is often simple for the movies to follow the original literary presentation of a detective story. But right here is the delicate issue: the ability of the camera to reproduce what in many novel plots is primarily the deductive ingenuity of the hero, the detective. If the story is a horror-thriller, this problem of communication does not exist. But the horror story has been exhaustively exploited for the sake of its unvarnished exposures of black and insinuating deeds; the machinery of crime has been nothing if not visible, and the identity of their perpetrator, if concealed, a mere formality. "X" usually marks the spot where the body lies, and it is seldom that the body disappears, though this is an inevitable adjunct of certain plots for the sake of complication.

Thus, while in works of art as the natural thing all is given, either explicitly or in the shape of more or less known symbols, an essential element is lacking to the nature of the mystery-detective story: the identity of the criminal and sometimes, as a necessary corollary, the method of the crime. The character of the detective mystery accordingly depends upon the omission of a main term that must be supplied before the story ends, in order to obtain the "total revelation" toward which all art proceeds. Technique of the detective mystery varies more than may be glibly supposed. First of all, the author delegates an agent of investigation, the detective, who proves his superiority to all other agents of investigation (notoriously, the police themselves). In my chapter on the villain and the hero, I did not emphasize the glorification of this "superman," for the particular reason that Hollywood has never realized the same heights with its straightforward solvers of crime as with its murderers and gangsters. One reason for this is obvious enough: the literary medium is more susceptible than the camera in displaying the deductive powers and mental ingenuity of the detective. The detective is a student—and according to fiction, a master—of psychology, and much of the form of the mystery narrative depends upon the detective's train of thought, which is followed approximately up to the end, when his final intuition of the criminal's identity is kept from the reader in order to save the conventional climax of the story—the sudden revelation of the criminal. Consequently, in the literary form, the consciousness of the detective hero is a specific convention which stands between the reader and knowledge of the criminal, in the course of discovering him, just as it stands between the detective and other persons in the story as a real obstacle. It is probable that, in the beginning, nobody knows the identity of the criminal excepting the criminal himself and his possible accomplices. The "game" is to guess his identity before it is revealed; thus, the reader is in some sense in competition with the detective. It happens, however, that owing to the nature of communication in the genre under discussion, the reader does not have the same chance as the detective, *who is on the scene.* In one sense, he may be argued to have a better chance, inasmuch as, unlike the detective as a rule, he is not under pressure of time, and so may go over "the evidence" as many times as he likes.

One thing must be noticed now. The presentation by cinema creates an *illusion of omniscience* which, under the circumstances, belongs correctly only to the detective. What I mean to say is that the camera, with its "literal" eye, is somewhat freer, in substance, to report what happens than is the verbal medium of literature. Notice that I do not say that the camera's ability to do this is used! That would not be Hollywood cricket. In other words, sometimes events, facial expressions, are shown to us (either reader or spectator) from which the detective is excluded. Yet such tantalizing "revelations" or clues must be deliberately selected, according to the discretion of author or director, and may be intended, indeed, as misleading—or "leading" in the sense of false lures. The fact remains that in the type detective-mystery, a subtle change of quality occurs when it is transferred from the printed page to the screen: the convention of the "knowing" hero, the detective, is damaged in the transference. Potentially, he is *all-knowing*, but in stepping out of a book into a Hollywood studio he relinquishes some of this potential faculty to the camera itself. All this is due to something which I have given great emphasis: the illusion of the screen's physical reality. Though it is quite possible to manipulate the spectator's psychology of suspicion and process of deduction in any number of tricky ways, both director and spectator are aware that in reproducing the physical conditions, the concrete *mise-en-scène*, the movies increase the *expectation of visual discovery which is the very heart of the detective mystery*. Either the screen must fulfill this in a peculiar way or fail to fulfill it in a conspicuous way.

There have been more than a few detective heroes whose exploits have been presented from time to time by Hollywood, notably Sherlock Holmes, Philo Vance, Ellery Queen, and latterly the Falcon and the Crime Doctor. The most popular Holmes movie, *The Hound of the Baskervilles*, had a great deal of hocus-pocus which the novel itself had designed to keep the reader in a state of thrill and suspense. This story is a good example of the crossbreeding of the two main divisions of detective story: the story of logical deduction and the story of horror (both done masterfully, of course, by Poe). Now the Hollywood camera is very much at home in the latter, but is somewhat stumped by the former. "Magically" disappearing persons, walls opening suddenly into secret passages, arms blossoming from apertures, and (since sound pictures) weird cries in the night—all these are incidental thrills of the rabbit-from-the-empty-hat kind. In all but the supernatural or pseudo-scientific yarns, such stunts create an appetite to learn not only how they are done but also the identity of the doer; sometimes, as in *The Gorilla*, the monster is a clever criminal in disguise. In fact, the more extravagant the melodrama, the more insistent the average spectator's curiosity as to who and how. The burden placed upon the movie is obvious: there must be a "debunking," whether verbal or visual. The material mechanism of the magician's tricks is revealed—even if only in a mental flashback by which a variety of effects are explained by a simple exposure of a fact or an identity. Under these conditions, the spectator may achieve a curious satisfaction. The subconscious mind of modern times entertains a perpetual yearning to be told that its deepest fears,

its wildest nightmares, are merely hocus-pocus, perfectly susceptible to the revelation of "daylight"—the
"light of reason." When we consider the almost limit-
less assortment of magicians' tricks, among which are
those of fake spiritualists, we can understand the vivid
rôle played by the camera in the solving of a mystery.
The camera has, indeed, had an important part in un-
covering the devices of fraudulent mediums. Thus,
there is a suspended faith in the mind of every spectator of a movie mystery that, *if only the camera be on
hand at the right moment*, the criminal will be revealed. Naturally, every spectator is aware that the
agent of curiosity and its satisfaction is *the human detective*, and that nothing will be solved without him.
But is it not the idiosyncratic defect of the professional
detective that mysteries are primarily man-made, consciously fabricated, and thus does he not conspire with
the rationalistic tendency just referred to in believing
all the horrors of nature and human nature are mere
nightmarish illusions? In *The Murders in the Rue
Morgue*, Poe's *rationalist* psychology made the criminal
an ape which had escaped from a menagerie—thus
setting him quite apart from the legendary and semi-
supernatural monsters of Gothic romance. Gothicism
—and, indeed, its descendant, surrealism—imply that
monsters, even if apparently they have an external
existence, are in some sense the meaningful creations

of man's brain, and dwell within him as well as out-side him.* Now, considering that Hollywood's natural impulse is to exploit horror and rapine, the story of logical deduction as an express form is automatically compromised by the cinema medium, and thus the rôle of its protagonist, the detective, rendered mate-rially ambiguous.

The problem with which any detective is faced squarely is this: What *type* of crime is the one he has to solve? He must determine the motive before he speculates on the probable identity of the criminal. Is it money or passion, or blended of both? He may embark on several different hypotheses and thus his suspicion may be attracted to several different people as the culprits. But if he be a really good detective, he has to keep one most crucial premise in mind; if he has to deal with a pathological case of crime, he must seek for clues which nature has planted for him and which have accrued over a number of years. Thus, he care-fully divides motive from method, though naturally, in respect to any single hypothesis of the criminal's identity, the method and the motive are inevitably parts of the same logical complex. The purpose of this little résumé is to show that two interwoven plots of the crime exist: the phenomenal plot of criminal nature, peculiarly suited to rendering by the camera,

---

* *The Cat People* is a fairly recent and an excellent, rare example of this principle of mystery.

and the character plot of the criminal individual, peculiarly suited to rendering by psychology—to the deductive faculty conventionally represented best by words. The shock-and-shiver melodrama of Hollywood combines these two plots in a childish way. But if we take the analogy of the fake medium, it is somewhat easier to perceive that the camera, by secret surprise or penetration of the dusky spiritualist ritual, reveals only the method by which such "frauds" are accomplished. It does not solve the "mystery" of their value to those who wish to believe in them. Thus it offers no light on the *natural mystery* of belief in supernatural phenomena, a belief which Hollywood subtly indulges even while it debunks it. We observe, too, that the camera is appropriate only when the most concrete symbolization of the rational faculty exists . . . as when the hollow hood of the gorilla's head is lifted off and we see a human face emerge from the rest of the costume.

Mr. Orson Welles is Hollywood's most straight-faced and ingenious gorilla, as well as its cutest. It is as though in *Citizen Kane*, Mr. Welles wished to make up for not having been born when his hero was born and thus been enabled to help create the history of the movies, which, as it turns out, he can only express in retrospect. Considered altogether apart from its literary fable, which I have discussed elsewhere in this book, the movie is monstrously clever, so much so that

Mr. Welles, as director and actor, is enabled to live a pseudo-historic agony of all the heroes and all the directors who ever commanded or participated in the operations of a movie studio. By utilizing all the stunt-devices Hollywood ever thought of—including the "intrepid" news shot of an "unphotographable" celebrity being wheeled around his private grounds in a chair—and by choosing a protagonist who blends many kinds of motive, Mr. Welles has arrived at a super-condensation, which appears in all its surrealistic glory once you lift the cellophane wrapping that embodies the ostensible fable. Even if you disengage the parts of this synthetic engine of cinema, you will get an inkling, because it is possible to lay side by side in your mind the newsreel, the comedy, the romance, the historical adventure, and the mystery story, all of which are in it. And note that the overall form is that of the detective story, and that outside the cellophane of the cinematic events is the ribbon of the news-reporter's search, the logical-deductive path, tied with a symbol of the "natural mystery": the word, "rose-bud." It is the word on the dying man's lips, and it occurs to a bright young reporter that here is a clue to the "enigma" of the dead man's life. His intuition, of course, is based on the myth of the meaning of "last words" in the mouths of the dying. This myth is founded on the moral-psychological premise that many persons go out of existence with some desire left

unexpressed or abortively satisfied, and that, in the
delirious irresponsibility of dying, this desire works
its way to the lips and achieves a momentary supremacy of form it never attained before. That Kane's
word is a to-be-identified symbol attests to Mr.
Welles' desire to be *everything* to his public, a writer
as well as actor and director.

Like all important devices, this little word reveals
more even than is on the surface of the mystery;
ostensibly, it is a mechanical device to allow the movie
to rehearse the dead man's life. But this "rehearsal"
(besides being something close to Mr. Welles' vora-
cious theatrical heart) is only the rehearsal which is
known in detective stories as the reconstruction of
the crime. For the reporter nominates himself as a
detective to track down the origin of the symbolic
word in Kane's life, which will reveal, so to speak,
the spot where "the body" of meaning lies in Kane's
fabulous outer existence. "Rosebud" is the X, the unknown quantity, which finally the camera must photograph. Thus Mr. Welles has at once combined the
simplest of devices with the most complex in a double sense: the clue is extremely simple, and so is its
physical explanation; but first we must follow the
logical-deductive path of the detective (which consists of a series of eliminations of probabilities) and
the natural-mystery path of Kane's life. The former
is represented—if not ably represented—by the reporter,

who altogether neglects the natural-mystery line of speculation; after all, he is only a reporter.

But this in itself is significant. For a reporter is someone who tries to get people to talk, simply by asking them or by deluging them with importunities, and his parallel in the detective world is the policeman, who tries to coerce answers from people. It is not that the people in Kane's life refuse to talk. Some of them talk freely, and indeed it appears that they tell all they know or remember. But this does not divulge what the reporter wishes to know—the import of the word, "rosebud." Why? For the simple reason, as we learn at the end, Kane has never disclosed this particular secret to anyone; if it signifies any rôle in his life, it is an unconscious rôle or a "Freudian" rôle. It has never been directly communicated. Mr. Welles' reporter may be said to suffer from the occupational delusion of inept playwrights and novelists, who believe (anachronistically, shall we suppose?) that all that is worth communicating is communicated by human nature *verbally*; or, in essence, *consciously*. The value given the peculiar timing of the word on Kane's lips was erroneously assumed by the reporter, who used the psychology of the policeman—namely, that a mystery is solved by a verbal confession which connects a dead body with its cause of death. The movie's assumption is that Kane is a spiritual dead body as well as a physical dead body, and that his spirit, in the sense of *happy spirit*, died when he was forced to part from his boyhood fetish, his sled, on which was written the name, "Rosebud."

Alas, the logic is ambiguous! And it conceals the clinic beneath the third degree—and beneath the clinic, the confessional. The sled "Rosebud" reaches an apotheosis in its "astral" appearance on Kane's lips, and the hero is cleansed at the moment of his death. Thus, starting with the religious confessional, the movie makes a psychoanalytical assumption and on this basis seeks a "criminal"—a masquerading culprit —after which, however, it proceeds to utilize the assistance of the detective-reporter, who seeks the possession of the mystery as though it were to be revealed in the manner of the charade—by connecting an object or objects with a word. The law itself, in all its majesty, is a charade in this sense. The crime occurs. As soon as the law knows how it occurs, all that has to happen from its subjective point of view is for someone to supply the name of the criminal or for the criminal to confess. The fun is over. The fun is definitely over in Mr. Welles' picture when the eye of the camera, meandering over the desolated pyramids of Kane's posthumous miscellany of bric-a-brac, at last hesitates and focuses on the sled being thrown into the furnace, and one sees the paint blister and the name "Rosebud" gradually vanishing on the surface of the wood. The apparently artless eye of the camera has "solved the mystery" where the human detective has failed. One faintly suspects, of course, that Mr. Welles is behind the camera. But this does not placate those who prefer the work of art to the charade.

According to the pattern of logical deduction, in which the reporter failed and in which the "impersonally" propelled camera succeeded, the criminal is the sled—namely, the criminal is the fact, the physical counterpart of Kane's spiritual agony; alternately, the fetish or the circumstantial evidence: Exhibit X. But now it is also a "dead body," in that it is the true identity of the dead man, the killed potential of his spirit. The spot has been duly marked with Mr. Welles' sensational "X," and the corpse cremated.

As an ambivalized quantity, however, "X" draws together the three patterns involving reluctant verbal communication: the religious confessional, the psychoanalytical clinic, and the legal third degree. What have these patterns in common which makes it possible for the symbolic sled to embrace them all? They invert cause and effect, since in each case the narrative *begins* with the phenomenon and proceeds to its explanation, *finishing* with the cause. The three methods of procedure recognize the mystery of the phenomenon as "guilt" and a redeeming or cancelling function in the elucidation of the mystery. This concept is crudest in the police court, where the name of the criminal and his resultant conviction is sufficient to erase the crime from the police records—if the crime remains unsolved or the prisoner pronounced inno-cent, a smirch remains on the books of the police, of science, or of God. Something has not been brought to the light, to "justice."

Let us glance at the structural efforts of Mr. Welles to provide such a justice for his hero's guilt. The truth is that in eliding so tightly the three patterns, there is insufficient room for them to breathe in: the whole plot is too trig, melodramatic, and charadish. No basis exists for the esthetic judgment of Kane's life accord-ing to the form given his story. A very significant thing remains: the fact that the hero's death occurs at the beginning of the screen narrative, inverting the tragic pattern of the hero's death at the end of the last act. He is revived in *Citizen Kane* ostensibly for the sake of discovering the meaning of the symbol, rose-bud. But neither meaning nor thing named is dis-covered—at least not by the traditional revealer of facts, the news-reporter who, in the rôle of detective, represents the force of human intelligence and justice. Mr. Welles quaintly reserved the privilege of uncover-ing the thing named to Hollywood's pet, the movie camera. This surrealist eye has been signally, narcis-sistically honored by one who likes to think of himself as a pet: the new, if already tarnished, Hollywood genius, Orson Welles. Where does the body lie in which Mr. Welles is really interested? Being in Mr.

Welles' own breast, its cremation is a charade. Like Carmen and her officer in the Chaplin version of the operatic story, the sled may be expected to emerge from the furnace whole, smile, and take its bows. Whatever it may be nicknamed, it is Mr. Welles' personal ambition. As for the other directors, they are "dead," and Mr. Welles is the rosebud who will make flower all that they have failed to realize.

With Hollywood's surrealist eye in his lapel, Mr. Welles has utilized the great tradition mentioned at the beginning of this book, that of displacement in the comprehensive scheme of values we identify as "reality"—the whole and balanced richness of human existence. Esthetically, Mr. Welles, even as his newsreporter does, intuits the existence of the natural mystery, but for convenience' sake, for the sake of a stunning and well-aimed success, he has preferred to make it a detective story charade—one of those "see how it's done, it's really very simple" mystery solutions. It is a "displacing" irony in the sense of the magician's fluent charade of ease, and Mr. Welles meant to displace with one gesture the classic reputations in the directorial hierarchy.

On the other hand, the truly sur-real irony is that photographing a thing well does not explain its meaning in the great context of values. "Rosebud" remains a thing, an inanimate object, a mechanism—alas, it cannot come back from death and take its bows! It is a trite kind of symbol, surely, a "skeleton in the closet." But the camera discovers it in the way a child points or opens its mind in public. The child-camera has been conceived by Mr. Welles as an adequate antidote for the closed-mouth reluctance of "inscrutable nature"! There is a certain sensationalism in the revelations made by children, especially when strangers are present, and a lot of strangers hide in the darkness of a movie theater. But is all nature to be conceived as a family with a few skeletons rattling in its cosmic closet? Art, in the genuine sense, has always been above the *documentary*, the *circumstantial*, evidence of reality unless its purpose has been consciously limited. *Citizen Kane* is a spectacular kibitz of the Hollywood charade with its mechanism glaringly and scandalously visible. A thousand Hollywood turkeys are served up on Mr. Welles' sled, and their putrescence measured with amazing olfactory accuracy and disposed of by decent incendiarism. But in another respect, the sled, the fetus, the potential instrument, has the faculty of the phoenix. The eye of the camera is still alive.

CHAPTER X

TO BE OR NOT TO BE;
OR, THE CARTOON TRIUMPHANT

MODERN life deals us many surprises and at a rapid rate of speed. Its very pace, even in time of peace, is hard on the nerves, and keyed-up city dwellers, avid readers of the scandals, murders, international developments, the comic-strip, and "Believe It or Not" departments are always prepared for the mental and emotional eye-opener. The values of Hollywood naturally have kept rhythm with the thickness and fastness of existence beyond its studio walls. Interesting to note is that the taste for rapid action used to be satisfied largely by horses, automobiles, and trains in the old Western and adventure serials. A good chase was one of the great stand-bys of Hollywood in supplying its film climaxes and is by no means outré today. The modern melodrama, depending equally on action but buttressed with many subtle resources, tries to make the rapidity of pace permeative and inward, to give a consistent snap to all levels of the story. Hitchcock, the English director, is an adept at creating "expectancy," his best film to date being *The Lady Vanishes*, which incidentally indulges with profit in some old-fashioned mystery hocus-pocus.

With the accent cleanly on *pace*, surprise is more or less prepared for, since desperation and inspired effort lead naturally toward danger, accidents, and the otherwise unforeseen. Hence modern movie audiences are natural patrons of the grotesque, the sudden twist of plot, or the surprise climax. Of course, they desire the surprise without cost to the underlying conventions in all their heavy multiplicity, a good portion of which has been indicated in past chapters. Yet again, it is Hollywood's perpetual wail that efforts at originality have always been sternly rebuked by popular taste, with few exceptions, and so the great puzzle of the movie city is to be both startling and banal at once . . . just as, indeed, it has to show that a woman is both good and bad, and that life ends and does not end.

If Hollywood were serious about the ambiguity of modern values, as it is not, *To Be or Not to Be*, starring Jack Benny and the late Carole Lombard, would have been a different story. The paradoxical title from Shakespeare is not accidental but one of those quaint clues of which Hollywood, on careful examination, is by no means ungenerous. The time has come when a sort of systematic chaos exists in Hollywood's proved esthetic values. It cannot be called surrealism, even of the Marx brothers, Olsen and Johnson, or Gracie Allen variety, because it is not witty; it is not verbal *Dada* or pantomimic farce with symbolic overtones. It is, however, a sort of *Hellzapoppin* version of Pirandello—though more profoundly incongruous even than this characterization hints. It should be borne in mind that at the bottom of artistic nonsense, from Rabelais to Gracie Allen, from *Alice in Wonderland* to Lautréamont, is a joy in wit for its own sake and a consciousness of power and freedom. The dominant force is the destructive image, willfully displacing reason and logic, and molding reality wholly into a violent and strange form, having its unique quality and aspect.

Now when Hollywood is violent and strange, it is "Gothic" and magical, but the emotional pattern (as in such fables as *Dr. Jekyll and Mr. Hyde* and *Frankenstein*) is clear and unmistakable; it is *horror*, it is the thrill of fear or lust. When it is goofy, in the *Hellzapoppin* and Marx brothers sense, the emotional pattern is also clear; it is laughter—the irresistible response to a stylized form of pantomime and verbal wit. But when Hollywood essays a *complicated* charade, as in *To Be or Not to Be*, when it cooks up a recipe for comedy with the strangest admixture of styles and plot-motifs, the emotional pattern can hardly be said to exist. Ernst Lubitsch was the director, though not the author, and in this movie can be pointed out a true example of the catastrophic in charade-supplying. It is fathered by dozens of authors, however elliptically, and is synthetic to such an extent that its charade-meaning is apparently derived from some language not locally known, perhaps Esperanto or Eskimo. At the same time, the movie's form does not prevent its bromides of situation and nuance from being palpable; indeed, they stick out of this film like wrecks on the mental sound-track of the script-writers.

Only peculiarly contemporary conditions could have produced a film in which—aside from directorial "touches"—sensibility and style are lacking to such a horrific and chaotic degree. The time and scene of the film are Poland just before and after the German invasion. A Polish actor, his wife, and troupe are about to present a play about the cruelties of Nazism. The film has been constructed like a series of magician's tricks, not new to the screen but here in large number. The initial eye-opener is the now familiar device of showing a scene apparently a direct part of the movie but which at a crucial point is revealed as a play within the movie. But in this particular "play within the play," the actors are obviously Hollywood comedians at their time-honored job of working up to a gag. The question the spectator instantly asks is: Is the Nazi play *within the movie* supposed to be unintentionally bad, and thus hammily funny, or are they intentionally acting the ham parts of those pigs, the Nazis? This illustration gives the key-value of ambiguity in this movie. Jack Benny fits perfectly into the scheme, but in regard to the casting, in his case one can also ask: Is Mr. Benny merely acting himself, his own radio charade, or was his behavior written in the script? Here that curious independence of style which now and again creeps into films was oddly apparent. *To Be or Not to Be* has the air of having been made up, like a charade, from scene to scene in the studio, with nothing definitely planned.

Yet as the plot develops, the dubious ambiguity proves remarkably consistent. The Polish troupe, especially Mr. and Mrs. Tura, its stars, become involved in an espionage situation in which they have to rescue papers from the Gestapo in order to save themselves and a large number of prominent compatriots; they are all in the underground Polish movement. Later, in order for the troupe to escape from Poland, they are compelled to enact the very rôles they were stopped from playing previously by the Gestapo's prewar threat. Mr. Benny, assuredly one of the world's least persuasive actors, comic or otherwise, impersonates one of the head spies, a Polish traitor, while another

cheese-faced member of the troupe plays a mute Hitler, looking precisely like a waxen apparition from
Madame Tussaud's. In the sense of device and twist
of plot, this is one of the trickiest of films, but there
is no awareness in it of dealing with that single and
readily recognizable "substance" known as life. No
matter how exaggerated artifice may be, it may be
symbolically recognizable; no matter how arbitrary
plot may be, it is possible to create an underlying
design, a symbolic unity. To make a list, *To Be or
Not to Be* is all of a Lubitsch sex comedy, a Hitchcock spy melodrama, an act of *Hellzapoppin*, and a
play about character-ambiguity by Pirandello, as the
whole might have been written by Clifford Odets in
an immoral moment. For a highly complicated dish
to be successful, either in cooking or art, an exquisite
taste is necessary. Hollywood possesses no such taste.
Sometimes the movie has the aspect of a second-rate
revue. Mr. Lubitsch can allow Jack Benny, dressed
like a Vassar girl as Romeo, to mince six or seven
steps away from the camera and then, seen face to
the audience, recite the first words of the "To be or
not to be" speech like a timid actress in the rôle of
Goethe's Marguerite. . . . In a comedy, it is necessary to take one thing seriously: the comedy. In this
scene, flatly speaking, Mr. Benny made me feel like
dying . . .

Yet is it not odd that the comedy in this film is not taken as "straight" as it should be; indeed, that nothing in it is quite straight? For this, there is a contemporary reason and, with respect to movie history, an ancient one. Give the charade a group of inexpert performers, and it becomes, willy-nilly, a cartoon—the most impertinent and nonchalant form of humor. The peculiarity of all political cartoons is that they are double-faced and to be distinguished in this sense from the "single face" of the caricature. Thus Hogarth, Rowlandson, and Daumier, and all social caricaturists, had a fundamental seriousness which, like Swift's, lay in their direct approach to man as a planetary animal. Mankind is evaluated by a few strokes of the pen or an epigram. But the cartoon, either the political cartoon or the less significant comic strips, such as *Gasoline Alley* or *The Gumps*, achieves a split of interest, either by being for one side against another or separating reality from romance. Its content is projected into a fairy-tale world, a sort of wish-fulfillment world, which says in effect: "Oh, if things were only like this, life wouldn't be a serious matter!" And the point of the caricaturing of the Nazi military man is "If Nazis were only like this, they wouldn't be a genuine menace!" But we know they are a genuine menace. The daily sacrifices of the American people, at home and on the battlefield, are no laughing matter. A dangerous and well-equipped adversary is in the field. Moreover, he is a respectable enemy in that overcoming him demands all our powers.

To view a picture such as *The Invaders*, recounting the fortunes of six members of a Nazi submarine crew who are marooned in Canada when the submarine is blown up by airplanes, was to be convinced of the tenacity of spirit and potent organization of Nazi forces. This film, astonishingly enough, reversed the rôle of the traditional romantic hero of Hollywood. No longer does the glamorous lone-wolf win out over tremendous odds. After he is deprived, one by one, of the little band, with a whole nation looking for him, the Nazi captain does not escape; he is captured by the wit and brawn of a Canadian private in an ingenious climax to his arduous saga. The film is English, and the actors starred in it take the parts of Englishmen and Canadians; they are all well known to the American screen: Raymond Massey, Leslie Howard, and Laurence Olivier. Yet these glamor boys take the "bit" parts; naturally, they are outstanding bits, and have the same place in the heroic values of the movie as a common man, a private in the army, would have should he distinguish himself by heroic action on the battlefield. So "life" has entered the hierarchy of Hollywood art and converted the conventional individualistic heroes into conspicuous members of the supporting cast—that "supporting cast" which is a figure of speech for the masses of the people. As cited in the chapter on John Doe, it is in the cards, however they be played, that all heroes must finally confess, by some means, that they are subject to the laws governing the man in the street. Historically speaking, gods and kings must be prepared to endure their periodic and ritual self-sacrifice; Garbo, the "goddess," had to become a mere woman, a client of American *couturières*. In comparison with *To Be or Not to Be, The Invaders* is a model of realism. Hollywood's general tendency is to present Nazis as caricatures participating in a struggle with "real people" having a highly developed sense of humor as well as an insurmountable cleverness. Melodrama and its tricks, used against the Nazis, become absolutely fabulous in *Mister V*, in which the situation is reversed. Mr. Howard, who is starred, is the professorial leader of a little band of archaeological students, and he effects the escape of twenty-eight important prisoners of the German police. Although in *The Invaders*, the Nazi captain had to face the most realistic opposition, Mr. V has to face only a comic-opera set of Gestapo agents. I do not complain of the facts, if they are facts. I am an American, and know what my interests are. I complain of the Hollywood moral. The triumphant cartoon of inverted heroism is not respectable art or respectable thought . . . The troupe of Polish actors in *To Be or Not to*

Be make a comic-opera escape of the most incredible kind.

The moral of this whole cartoon, after a few moments' serious thought, is obvious enough. It is the aim of Hollywood, as of official propaganda, to separate the facts in the newspapers from the "facts" in entertainment. The psychology is that, if imaginatively the enemy is underrated, it is easier to defeat him. Is this true? Why is *To Be or Not to Be* so fabulously comedic and so incongruously put together? Is it not because even the Hollywood propagandists are aware of the profound dislocation required for, first, separating the hero from his *individualistic* function, and, second, separating the seriousness of life from the comedy of art? Granted that it is serious to treat sex from a farcical standpoint, because sex itself has, appropriately, a comic side of its own, still, by exaggerating this angle, we are brought around again to the seriousness of sex. By winning exemption from the tension of sex in a comic explosion, we are better prepared to grapple with its tension once more. But can the same argument be applied to the cartooning of Nazism?

Chaplin's personality gave a genuine caricature to Hitler's personality; he communicated to this characterization something of what he really was and gave the part a pathos which humanized Hitler. At several points in *To Be or Not to Be*, a commentator's voice is interpolated with regard to the appearance on Warsaw streets of a man taken for Hitler, and, later, the same voice describes the first bombing of the city. Why was this special device deemed appropriate? Did it not seek to provide a place in the movie for such a serious thing as a bombing, a note which is exceptional to the comic pattern of the plot? It seems self-evident and is also tangible proof that the movie is aware of its inconsistency as a pastiche. Now, here a fact is introduced into a work of art—a very recognizable fact: the bombing of cities. And side by side with it is the attitude recommended by Hollywood art. Should art itself adopt defensive measures? Was "art," too, caught "unprepared"? If Hollywood, in the pictures just noted, has organized some of its heroes as "underdogs" and its "underdogs" as glamorous lone-wolves, it is because social morality itself has been caught in a defensive posture. It is thus peace, and the art and morality of peace, which have been unprepared.

We must face the fact that the typical American hero has been placed in the anomalous and rather embarrassing position of becoming, at times, a sort of Mickey Mouse, just as "the enemy" is a Frankenstein's monster whose power is based on "inferior" mechanical insides. Mickey is a David who is heroic through the ingenuity of his mechanical weapons.

But why should Americans fall so easily into the postures of the underdog? Isn't the United States a
powerful and large nation? Doesn't the British Empire
cover almost two-thirds of the globe? It is *Germany*
that is relatively small. Yes, but it has become large
through the upstart genius of fascism, a philosophy
of the Great Leader against many scattered groups of
small leaders. The most famous myth of Hollywood
has come true—in Berlin! The bandit, the "Robin
Hood of the Aryan Race," robs the "rich" of the
world to give to Germany which, according to this
legend, is the "poor" of the world. For its "sins" of
glamorizing the public enemies and the Little Caesars,
at first moralistically and then nonchalantly, Hollywood is now paying the rapidly minted and dubious
coin of its art. Values have to be hastily rejuggled.
The script writers are sent scuttling to their dens to
rewrite a third rewriting. There must be laughs.
There must be patriotism. There must be all this—
and hell, too . . . but a censored hell, a neat hell, a
sugared hell.

It may be argued that democracy on the defensive
has to organize all its resources to fight and finally
conquer the enemy. If so, that is too bad. I do not
deny it may be true. But in this bitter fact, this radical
state of affairs in which art must be sacrificed, are not
some of us to remain critical? Are we not to record

what is happening in the *factual* sense to art? If an incendiary bomb punctures the ceiling of our apartment, we instantly adopt a critical attitude toward the event and attempt by proved methods to quench or smother it. Can we not do the same for art? Taste, standards of judgment, the maintenance of a serious morality, these are not mere traits of unusual individuals. Under democracy, they tend to spread, to be assimilated by the many. Hollywood has been a great but whimsical educator, sometimes even a force of obstruction and perversion. Yet art has always had its popular aspects, and Hollywood has produced a few great works. It is the admirable exceptions of Hollywood for which I implicitly speak in this book. I have also spoken, as I declared at the outset, for those irresponsible wonders of the movie city, those uncoördinated and inadvertent elements of grandeur, which it affords along with all the frippery and the falsity. An exceptionally equipped spectator is required, on the other hand, to discern and evaluate these chance events. One of the Janus faces of Hollywood must be saved, but it must be the one with eyes on the future. Mr. Benny is a gag man. His face must go. He is not responsible—not even for his gags. He distorts *To Be or Not to Be* exactly the way the claim (which was featured in *Mister V*) that Shakespeare is a native ancestor of Nazi culture distorts the true and unique face of reality. Mr. Lubitsch's film itself is full of remarkable effects of melodrama and even some genuine wit. Not only is pace absent, however, but all is spoiled by a hamminess that infects the whole as a single drop of sour milk infects sweet milk. Is this way, finally, "to be or not to be"? It is the privilege of Americans to answer with an emphatic negative. Perhaps we will get around to it. If we do, Hollywood will obey. What else can it do?

It is, moreover, the principle of the thing. As to the sometime fact, Hollywood is quite capable of putting its ear to the ground and reading official prognoses and warnings in the newspapers; vide, the recent Lifeboat directed by Hitchcock. Obviously, here, a highly capable German enemy must be defeated by the scions of democracy. But the lesson is not so allegorical in nature as many have supposed. In the lifeboat, the Nazi is literally outnumbered. Eventually, numerical power is bound to win, and we have the numerical power on every level, in every department. Yes! Nazism will be pushed overboard. Just as inevitably as that. But meanwhile, the succession of sins against art and reason will have been pasted by Hollywood on the billboards of history.

CHAPTER XI

THE HUMAN MASK

In Chapter II, I wrote this sentence concerning a primitive stage in the development of movie technique: "The point was not that actors should express emotions with their faces, but rather the reverse, that they should express their faces with emotions—to prove they were real, not wax-works, faces." Since movie photography and make-up now leave no doubt that we are watching real faces on the screen, we might think that emotion is no longer called upon to express the mere reality of the human face, and that all the actor's face must do is to express emotion. Perhaps the most striking irony about Hollywood is that its art still lags in this respect: the actor's face very seldom forms a character mask; that is, it seldom conveys the mature experience of an adult, rarely lends authority to the words with which an actor expresses his emotions.

This point may be obviously illustrated. The term,

"character," in Hollywood primarily means the assumption by an actor of a *different* or *older* character. Merle Oberon and Barbara Stanwyck become "character actresses" by portraying rôles that take them from youth to old age. Paul Muni, and formerly Lon Chaney, have assumed a varied assortment of rôles, not merely, in the former's case, because he could command—however dubiously—almost any accent, but also because both were inspired make-up artists: they invented masks for themselves. Muni's most ingenious mask was undoubtedly "Scarface." Hollywood has a fundamentally puerile conception of the *mask* as a disguise of character, whereas from the true esthetic viewpoint, the mask should reveal character.

But what, indeed, is "character" in the orthodox acting sense? It is the identity assumed by a personality for a particular rôle. In Hollywood, however, there has always been a gallery of personalities who may be called, in the popular sense of the word, "characters," and who were imprisoned in the masks provided for them by nature as surely as though each morning they had left their dressing rooms made up for a single rôle. Such types easily come to mind: Wallace Beery is one; Marie Dressler and Zasu Pitts, others. For a while, Mr. Beery was given "villain" parts, but the essentially comic pattern of his face at last triumphed. All three are memorable human masks because they belong to a semi-grotesque category;

indeed, they are contemporary masks of the comic, like the pre-eminent one of Charlie Chaplin, although his is an invention. The important thing about a "mask" is that, in itself, it is unchanging. If, however, the mask has a native "character interest," expresses some unique and revelatory quality of the human, it changes by remaining the same thing: it sheds light on everything with which it comes into contact. It is, exactly, a source of light. The unhappy thing about Hollywood acting is that most players, lacking the maturity of human experience before they face a camera, have to gyrate with their features in order to express feelings and ideas with emphasis.

I do not mean (as the reader knows quite well by this time) that Hollywood charades usually succeed in providing actors with really adult material to express. But my point will be evident by glancing at the technique of acting in French films. Take such talented actors as Louis Jouvet, Harry Baur, and Raimu. Jouvet acted in *The End of a Day* and Raimu in *The Baker's Wife*, two of the most beautiful films ever produced. Interesting to note is that Raimu is a "French Wallace Beery"; both, roughly speaking, are "common man" types. But we instantly notice that Beery is coarser, and that both his "human mask" and acting technique lack the finesse of Raimu's. By American standards, Jouvet's style and, for instance, that of Victor Françen, are "wooden." The fact is

that this supposed woodenness is the effect of the
immobility of their "masks," the unchangingness of
their facial expressions. This unchangingness is not to
be confused with monotony. On the contrary, a style
adopted by French actors for high-comedy and drama,
it shadows forth a subtle variety.

In *The End of a Day*, there is an interesting example of a comic mask, a male actor's corresponding
to the extravagant features of the deceased actress,
Edna May Oliver. Yet this actor did not gyrate his
features the way Miss Oliver used to gyrate hers. The
reason is simple: the French actor's comedy was prin-
cipally in his lines—the lines of the play, not the lines
of his face. The comic mold of his face merely
emphasized the comic nature of his rôle, whereas in
Miss Oliver's case, her effect depended entirely upon
her facial and bodily pantomime apart from the significance of her lines. Being by no means the same
thing as "character," what is the "human mask" in
acting?

It is the un-cinematic element of the cinematic. It
is what is already given in *human* personality before
the individual personality is assumed. It is as immobile
as a painting is. This is why Garbo fascinated us by
her presence alone. The mold of her face expresses
without having to move; so does Mae West's; so did
Duse's and Bernhardt's. Louis Jouvet's face, no matter
what rôle he plays, expresses a certain sum of human

experience that resides in the modulations of his face as lines of print reside in a novel. It is a quality which, unhappily, very few actors in Hollywood possess. I cannot think of an American actress who has it to any notable degree. First of all, American actors are all too young. It was a relief to welcome, among the Hollywood male leads, the dissipated face of Joseph Cotten. On the other hand, Orson Welles has a childish type of countenance which makes him an unsuitable mask for any but peculiarly neurotic adult rôles, and yet he is too big to play adolescents. This condition drove him into inventing masks for himself. Edward G. Robinson is the only dramatic actor mature in years who possesses a really striking mask, but then Mr. Robinson (doubtless owing to his experience in gangster rôles) has mugged himself into a permanent grimace. Walter Pidgeon is a mature actor who never mugs, but he looks much too much like Walter Pidgeon. Alone among the serious American actresses, Bette Davis creates an illusion of the mask; I phrase it this way, because the whole effect of the mask comes from her eyes, which are hyperthyroid in tendency. Their restlessness keeps her face in constant, too constant movement. This means merely that her personality, as I stated at length in a previous chapter, is neurotic. Neuroticism is something, but it limits, at the same time that it defines, the mask.

Before the talking movie appeared, American actors

had a better chance to create their "human masks."
Not only did we get Chaplin then, but also Lillian
Gish, as well as the romantic figures of Rudolph
Valentino from Italy and John Barrymore from Broadway. Acting, with distinct but rare exceptions, was
extremely bad in the first two decades of the movies.
Of course, in Hollywood less was demanded of acting
than on the stage. At the same time, because everything depended in those former times, so far as the
actor went, on pantomime, the actor's physical style
had to be highly distinguishable, had to have some
of the quality of the human mask. If nowadays we
notice a relatively competent young actor, such as
Robert Young, we see that physically he has no style
whatsoever. Yet if we recall certain matinee idols of
the older days, such as Carlyle Blackwell and Eugene
O'Brien, we see acting much less competent than
formerly, but we see something more important: a
sense of physical style, a sense of fulfilling certain
functions merely by being an image, even if the only
objective were to cause the most commonplace flutter
in the feminine heart.

As we know, great art is simple; its simplicity is
subtle, never stark or crude. What I described in "The
Technicolor of Love" as the ability of actors and
actresses to reveal, "to denude," by the simplest movements of the clothed body, may have a great simplicity. Provokingly enough, Hollywood's art does not

have to be greatly simple to obtain extraordinary effects. Vivien Leigh as Scarlett O'Hara and Leslie Howard as Ashley Wilkes are not great masks, but they become extraordinary chiefly through the magic machinery of Hollywood. Carlyle Blackwell's romantic profile and black hair, his genteel slouch, fashionable with men at that time even though it produced a visible belly, formed a significant hieroglyph and is part of the romantic tradition of the movies. Valentino's arrival meant an influence of fire, and gave a content to the artificial athleticism of Fairbanks, Senior. Valentino had charm and zest, and even the addition of John Barrymore's profile to the screen gallery did not challenge the former's supremacy as a romantic type. The human mask, finally, is the complete physical style of an actor, and exists independently of the special character he plays.

Just as Valentino's face, smiling or unsmiling, conveyed an "ocean of meaning" to spectators, so latterly did Dietrich's for her sex. Dietrich, fully clothed, is far more alluring than Betty Grable or Dorothy Lamour, divested of all but their modesty. It is a sad fable, especially sad to be so popular, that "mystery" is inseparable from "the dark," that *to be mysterious is to be concealing.* Even mystery, to exist, must expose its symbol, evince its inviting hieroglyph. The most moving among mysteries are invariably those that brazenly reveal their masks to the light. The human presence is literally a *mask* for all the experience the human being has undergone. So the Human Mask is the face or "façade" symbolizing one human experience. To have great acting, there must be great masks, too.

CHAPTER XII

THE DAYLIGHT DREAM

$\mathbf{D}_{\text{AY}}$ and night. What exotic dreams! The most daring romantic dream man ever had was to create a bright and saturative light after the sun had withdrawn its holy essence from half the planet. A rival sun; an artificial light. What a candle for the universe! It is as though the moon, believed dead, had been unscrewed from the socket of heaven and brought down to be placed behind a small transparent picture, so that a great hallucination was created on an empty space—the empty space of night whether it is black or white. The most primitive movies were created by placing a lighted candle behind opaque silhouettes cut from paper—we get the same effect when we place our hands in front of a light and create figurations on a blank wall. Of course, it is the spirit of night that moves in our fingers, and the light is still, as steady as the sun. This light is necessary for projection, for reproduction after cinema is created. Primitive cinema was done in black on white on the gyroscope, a contraption that whirled like the earth in space: a horse ran, a man leaped. Then, when the camera reproduced this physical principle by unwinding film in front of what it was desired to photograph in movement, light was necessary, sunlight and then intense artificial illumination. And the same intensity was necessary for the *reproduction* of the moving images as was required for their *recording.*

The eye had absorbed the exterior light falling upon opaque masses, a dialectic which created space—the eye of the camera: the lens and the film. Then, bringing to its aid the artificial light, the lens and the film could project what had been memorized. But for this, certain conditions, conditions of rest and darkness were necessary. We are obliged to forget our immediate concerns when we enter a movie theater and relax in our seats. What we remember, for reasons given throughout this book, is apt to be rather accidental and associated with states of passive memory, with moments of daydreaming and spontaneous wishing. Hence the darkness of the movie theater is actually the night itself, the night of sleep and dreams. And the field of the screen is the lidded eye through which the mind that will not sleep, the universe whose sun will not go down, projects its memory and its wild intelligence, penetrating unnumbered relativistic miles into empty space to reach . . . immeasurable trivia. Trivia? Much has been said about Hollywood's trivia, about the strange relativism of size which pervades its studios and its creations.

I have defined this relativity in many ways, in various directions. But it is most necessary not to forget the machine and its rôle: the man-created element. For light, used for the purpose of illumination, and not for warmth or cooking, is an artifice, once it exists beyond the primitive forest, suited chiefly for the mental and spiritual needs of man. It was necessary for early man, surrounded by hostile animals and unprotected by walls, to build fires to scare off his enemies. Fire was also used in innumerable rituals, as a fetish against danger, as an exultation, as an accessory of sacrifice to the divine elements. And fire is but the red heart of light. In the heart of the earth, there is presumed to be fire, and in the heavens there is presumed to be an icy blue of vapor, so that the color gamut goes from red to yellow to green to blue, as we think of ourselves as vertical in relation to the earth's surface. And within this color gamut we must not forget the yellow burning to white to icy blue of daylight—artificial light, electric light. It is man's particular bright dream, for with it came thought, came reflection. After fire, after burning faggots, had served all the practical needs of his life, man cooked his mind over the symbolic fire of the night and achieved the concept. As white heat is necessary for the projection of what the camera's eye has memorized, it is also necessary for what man wishes to project on the screen of his memory, developing there as it issues from the sun of his brain. Around him, meanwhile, is the night, unseen but alive and moving, and existing in all its secrets and its phenomenal stories. To think that artificial light at first meant the scholar, the artist, the witchery of thought! Today, it means an extension of life for the purpose of a different kind of activity, for amusement, for courtship, for the vestiges of religious ritual (dancing and singing), as well as for study and artistic creation. Who is the artist in relation to this scheme, the Hollywood artist, as well as the painter and the poet? It is he who uses the daylight hours not for work in the common usage of the word, not for making the wheels of physical life go round, but for creating a product presumed either to amuse or uplift man in his "idle hours."

It is only natural for ritual, too, to go on an eight-hour-a-day working basis in this era of extreme specialization. The ritual of the daydream at night, of which artificial illumination is the symbol, cannot be abandoned merely because of the "daylight-saving" philosophy of bourgeois capitalism. What is religion? Is it not strictly speaking the spiritual illumination of the dark? God was created as the neo-spirit of the dark, for first He had to exist in order to set the sun in the heavens. Hence God is essentially the night, but He is also light-bringing. And man wishes to imitate Him, for light-bringing is in every way beneficial to the conditions on his earth. Yet the energy of man as an individual organism is limited; he must exile the light and return to the night from which he came in order to refuel the engine of his body and arise in the morning refreshed. *He must sleep.* But it happens that as man's brain has developed and provided a white sort of heat that rivals the heart, the brain too has its *langueurs,* its rhythms and rest periods, parallel orders of existence which do not coincide exactly with his expenditure of physical energy. Because of this *rivalry* between the bodily orders of existence in man, because of this economic inequality of energy elements within the human animal, the dream was created as the reverberation of an unconscious dissidence, the voice of desire for a more exact chiaroscuro. The dream is a bright-blowing flag, peopled with the enigmas of the future: future time and future space. The dream is that trembling flower which is a pure protest; it is the only pure and trembling flower of protest.

We know that even the burning eye of an electric bulb has a pulse, but a pulse whose throbbings are so finely separated that they beat in rhythm with the visual pulse, those waves of recognition by which the human eye envelops all that lies in the field of its vision. Of course, the eye is only a medium, a medium for light. The eye itself, as a physical engine, is nothing without the human intelligence, the light behind it. And within the human intelligence lies memory, a steadily burning if muffled light. The heart beats in sleep; the heart does not cease. The heart is the internal symbol of the human body, representing the world outside like an ambassador from a foreign country. At night it becomes a film behind which is placed the artificial bulb of the brain—a single bulb burning in the endless night of the body. Sometimes this body of the heart, like a planet in space, passes opaquely between the lower human body and the brain, and the brain is eclipsed. *This* is the dream. It casts the interior of the body into a dusk, a semi-seeing, lit by a fugitive flash. This is still the dream. Otherwise, in what we call "sound sleep," the heart is a mechanical thing, a remote thing; it is the veritable *illusion of the moon*, that cold celestial illusion produced in space by the hidden sun.

Light invaded the night. The man of cities lives on in his waking state after the sun goes down. He goes into the movie theater to be amused and moved, to feel that life is real but not very earnest, or else not very real and hence too earnest to bother about. Man robbed the night of its darkness in manifold ways. Was the night not going to retaliate according to the great inexorable law of its nature? It is enough for the night to entertain day, to submit to that eternally, rhythmically suppurating cancer in its black heart, the sun. Just as the mechanism of the body does not cease when the mind sleeps, but throbs till the organism awakes, so man as he works in field and factory and office behaves as the heart of what he has created, the things of his man-made world. In this world of bread-winning, even while he submits to the bargain he has made with his things, he himself—a little universe of light and dark, heat and cold—is sleeping, in a sense, working at sub-par, because in his interior universe, he reserves the right to shine at his utmost, and when he is acting like a machine among machines, he does not shine at his utmost, he does not create daylight in himself.

The world of mechanical things is a night, and the brightest metal, like the brightest blood when it passes beneath the lid of the eye, cannot shine in this night. The factory worker polishes his metal; he admires his metal; he knows it is part of a necessary night. He works, during war, longer than normally in this night, merely to create instruments that will destroy the enemy, annihilate the daylight of the enemy. And as, at night, the never-dark brain, the unshut eye, burns futilely through the opaque masses of the human body, man's spirit burns as futilely through the material objects which he has mechanically organized. It is himself, a sun amidst the sleeping world of things,

which creates the moony highlight on a piston rod,
no less than this highlight is created by the light of
the sun shining in the heavens. But this eye of memory, infused with the light of the brain, is as aware
of the night of the machines as the sitter in the movie
house is aware of the night of the world when his
attention is concentrated on events unreeling a hundred feet away on the screen. And sitting in offices or
standing in factories, repeating the same motions over
and over, speedily and flawlessly, the daylight dreamer
has his dream in relation to which the most glittering
machine is only a figment of primeval darkness.

Hollywood is but the industrialization of the mechanical worker's daylight dream. Do not think that
the vast factories of the movie city represent anything
more than the daylight dream, the dreamlight of the
soul and will and intelligence which is separated from
the night of things—the daylight dream extended
ritualistically into those hours reserved by custom for
relaxation and amusement. The compulsiveness of the
movie habit is neither simple nor limited; it has power
even over those who escape from intimate concern
with the wheels of the material world. For after all,
such an escape is in great part an illusion—as though
we could escape from the dark. The best we can do is
to isolate ritually the dark from the light. Few of us
are so free of obligation to the mechanical, objective,
and material aspects of living that we do not need to

reproduce our slavery to them, however partial, by slipping into a movie house and seeing unroll the most highly systematized, the commonest, daydream of all: the average Hollywood product. Is it not highly amusing, even to the weariest and most jaded of us, to observe the daydream, sought desperately in the blackest part of things, converted by the movie into the most logical forms of narrative, the most conventionalized of emotions, the most luminous shapes of the visible? For here is "reality," the rationally arranged, sensible orders of existence reproduced in the most literal and physical form possible to artifice. The "absolutism" of dream, its lawlessness in the Freudian sense, is here replaced by a formalized scheme available not merely to this or that individual but also to the person sitting next to him in the subway and the theater. Hollywood is the mass unconscious—scooped up as crudely as a steam shovel scoops up the depths of a hill, and served on a helplessly empty screen. A thousand small wishes are symbolically satisfied by the humblest and worst Hollywood movie, and the excellence or triteness of a movie has little to do with satisfying the average customer. He goes to see it as to a sacrifice rather than as to a celebration. Pain, theoretically, is to be mixed equally with pleasure, and one is as welcome as the other. Surely the sadism, no less than the masochism, of this book has not been missed by the reader. The act of submitting to the spell of a movie is to me a ritual of masochism, while writing about my experiences in the movie theater is a ritual of sadism. The impulse of the daydreamer is to escape from the facts. The artist always begins by being a daydreamer, but his daydreams are inevitably turned into works of art by way of the dialectic of testing them by relating them back to the facts. This movement is continuous. Facts, to the artist, form an opacity, and the concept of opacity is black, relieved only by light, which provides a conception of the object in space, a conception of the total relations of living processes. Translucency is mental, a reading of the future, purely a question of learning the formula of total action. Science is translucent by divining the mechanical insides of things, the will which exists in a single element contributing to larger complexes, but science's mentally disintegrating eye, soon discovering that "singleness" is relative, has divided and subdivided until the atom, and beyond-the-atom, has been split. It is very hard to relate such a vast number of active elements as science describes back to a simple human need, a concrete human desire: the need for sleep and food, the desire to love and be happy. Hence, science's burning eye, while it creates vast abstract structures, tends to show that in relation to the total physical world, with man as its center, such structures might as well be made of cellophane. It is as necessary for science to be humanly modest as it is for art to be humanly pretentious, and Hollywood is art at its most humanly pretentious; and, thus, I hint at its necessity.

Today, Hollywood is as necessary as our economic *status quo*, and no more and no less necessary. In a day of modern painting and literature, the exploration of the dream and, coevally, of the far past of mankind, there are many references to the monstrous. The home of the monster is perennially in man's brain, for there the monster is first illuminated and burns only in intimate contact with the womb whose sperm is the light of memory—that memory which, contrary to its orthodox reputation, is as inventive as it is passive. It is only when man wills it so that memory is conceived as passive, as faithfully reconstructive in the logical narrative sense, as producing a well-balanced concept of total experience. Proust's great novel, to which I have referred previously, is a remembrance of things past on a specific basis of what occurred in a *selected* past. Indeed, Proust's actual novel is a "Hollywoodizing" of what really occurred, an adaptation on the basis of the most discreet, overt, and palatably memorized eventuations. True, it consists of the way Proust most nearly thought of these things from an esthetic viewpoint at the time when he experienced· them. But this is merely the novelist's method of composition and, being a specific method, must exclude as well as include certain kinds of truth. Sometimes Hollywood too tries to treat life, as feasibly as possible, the way some great author treated it, but the charade produced, and presented on thousands of theater screens, is basically a selective, and thus more or less unconsciously censoring, method of composition. I hope I have not given the impression that the conception of charade is totally foreign to legitimate literature. Proust's novel is a charade of Parisian society played in the intimacy of his bedroom, while he himself is confined to his bed alone. While all things may enter the darkness of the bedroom, some are excluded from the brightness of the bedroom. Some things we do are really done in the dark, in semi-dark, or perforce under fugitive streaks of light, fugitive visibility—it is the shocking effect of these fugitive glimpses, knit with such profoundly intimate emotions, that so often distort our visual perspectives and create those purely emotive forms seen in modern and primitive types of painting. But Proust depended, as Hollywood depends, upon a decently burning light in the bedroom no less than in the drawing room; upon the classical traditions of form characteristic of the whiteness of Greek marble figures no less than of the light that burned so equally in the minds of Plato and Euclid, illuminating the whole human house by a single beam. This is also what the movie projection machine attempts to do: cast a straight beam throughout the world's house. That is why I think of Hollywood actors and actresses as gods and goddesses in the Greek sense, images always seen (virtually) at full length, composed and in relaxed attitudes, whether sitting, standing, or reclining. A popular actress dare not distort her face too much. Tales are told of the rages of goddesses, but one never sees Minerva in a temper or Venus' face contorted with jealousy (unless in a modern French movie), for if one did, they would seem almost monstrous. The monster is the son of light and darkness; he is part day and part night; part reason and part blind desire—but beware of the proportion and its occasion! In seeking amidst the past and the present like grab bags, Hollywood has produced out of ignorance the proportions of the monster.

But this ignorance—what is it but the deliberate, systematized exclusion of knowledge which results from man's efforts to adjust himself to the external world, the world of sunrise and sunset, as simple as the raising or lowering of a shade? But does not such a "natural" simplicity depend entirely on what happens between sunrise and sunset, the way in which darkness and light have been timed, opacity and translucence manipulated? Ah, there are "standards" for these things, just as there is "standard time" and "daylight-saving time." Such criteria, in the dynamic sense, are utilized by men to be conventional, to coöperate, fuse, and harmonize with their environment, large or small. In Hollywood, this element is placed side by side with a bold creative attempt: the creation of the visual language of the films; an art of representation which creates specific cinematic means, a means grown so much larger than the dynamic ability of the content. So does the dynamic power of the individual often outpace his desire to be conventional, to fit in, to render his desires "normal" in every way. Out of *this* individual comes the artist or the scientist, someone with a creative technique—a technique derived entirely from *preoccupation with the daydream*. Hollywood is in competition with other forms of art; it, like the artist, wishes to outshine rival artists. But, as I have tried to show, it is composed internally of an aggregate of rival artists, a structure of elements designed to create a highly popular, undifferentiated series of products, and is also competitive, compromising, building on destruction. In this sense it is too much of a social science, too little of a social art. The black daylight of the office and the bright nightlight of the movie theater balance too easily the daydream of the office and the night dream of the theater; the effect is one of *cancelling*, and hence of a perpetual suspension of the true conflict of forces.

The thesis of Hollywood, the personal daydream of the common man, is suspended in its antithesis, the mass daydream, and cannot break out of this womb.

The movie theater is the psychoanalytical clinic for the average worker and his day-, not his *night*, dreams! He emerges from the theater cured of the illusion that his effort to alienate himself from the night of mechanical work in lighted office or factory is morbid, a monstrous kind of wish. By seeing it re-created, formalized, conventionalized on the screen, he is immeasurably reassured; he is healthy again. What do his night dreams matter? He has roughly equated in his mental continuity the facts of his night and those of his day. He has reached a classical adjustment: *the gods do it, too.* The gods are like him; they too are sentimental, frustrated, escapist. They too seek fine clothes —wine, women, and song. But *they* are contented. They are paid. Their agonies are sham. That is the priceless faculty of the divine; they earn their livelihood by being themselves—just by being themselves. A celestial, a socialist Utopia? Let man go forth and imitate them. Let him be reconciled. Let the end of desire be its beginning. Let the night of the machines descend on him every morning at eight-thirty. All right, he will dream. But his dream will be psychoanalyzed in the evening. Let him pierce this night with images of pleasure and longing, dreams of the flesh and the soul; he will see those dreams ritualized and "realized," equated with the mechanical night in the inside of the movie theater.

But this is barren. All the monsters of Hollywood

cannot compare with the luminous and authentic monstrosity of a little child's drawing or the paintings of the insane. For in these lie the basic sperm of the creative dream, the desire to bring light into darkness, and so transform both. I do not mean by this a logical compromise, a formal, gray reality, for in its ceaseless movement, human desire can never stop to become a logical fusion, a static neutrality of coloration. Human desire is to pierce the deepest dark, no matter how remote it may be. From this: a synthesis—an explosion, a restless rainbow of color—an all-consuming, all-creating dialectic! The movement of light into space is endless and revolutionary. Today, science tells us that the behavior of the universe is far more complex and "unreadable" than materialist science has declared it to be. Some of science's most cherished principles have fallen by the wayside, have died, while some of the most ancient myths have survived. The movement of the planets exists, we believe, and laws have been invented that explain the seasons and day and night themselves by computing the manner in which the rotating earth circles the sun. However complex this system is, it becomes fabulously simple when we consider the moon of lovers, the sun of bathing beaches, the seasons of grain-growing, the evening of the supper bell, and the morning of the alarm clock. We do our best to obey the laws of nature in conjunction with the functional structures of our society. But the sun, the moon, the stars, and the earth as we know them—either as classical myths or scientifically defined bodies—are not the only spheres possible. Nor are the colors on the simple palette the colors of the artist's picture. The imagination has transformed them. No matter how bright technicolor may be, it is too dark if it hangs there, a chimera in a void, unattached to a dominant imagination, unleashed to the forces that are really carrying us to the wide world's end and beyond. Through the camera's eye, Hollywood has developed a tremendous faculty for the presentation, however inadequate, of the classical-humanist world of men and women. Inherent in its visual realism lies the irreducible tag of the human norm, that "armature" on which mankind must work its future miracles. Hollywood can remain monstrous and pernicious in its varieties of hallucination or be seriously utilized, I hazard, toward an end beyond what any other art has accomplished in a mass sense. Now that, with the rest of cultural manifestations, the movie city's works are being placed on a universal testing ground, we shall see what happens to the camera, to the charade, to "displacement," and to "reality." After all, everything proceeds by contradiction. That is our intrinsic social hope.